IT'S A WONDERFUL WORD

By the same author

Red Herrings and White Elephants
Shaggy Dogs and Black Sheep
Phantom Hitchhikers and Decoy Ducks
Loch Ness Monsters and Raining Frogs
Pop Goes the Weasel
The Old Dog and Duck
What Caesar Did for My Salad

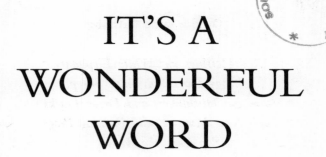

IT'S A WONDERFUL WORD

The Real Origins of Our Favourite Words,
from Anorak to Zombie

ALBERT JACK

Illustrations by Ama Page

BOOKS

Published by Random House Books 2011

2 4 6 8 10 9 7 5 3 1

Copyright © Albert Jack 2011
Illustrations © Ama Page 2011

Albert Jack has asserted his right under the Copyright, Designs
and Patents Act, 1988, to be identified as the author of this work

First published in Great Britain in 2011 by
Random House Books
Random House, 20 Vauxhall Bridge Road,
London SW1V 2SA

www.randomhouse.co.uk

Addresses for companies within The Random House Group Limited
can be found at: www.randomhouse.co.uk/offices.htm

The Random House Group Limited Reg. No. 954009

A CIP catalogue record for this book is available from the British Library

ISBN 978 1 84794 669 0

The Random House Group Limited supports The Forest Stewardship Council (FSC®),
the leading international forest certification organisation. Our books carrying the FSC
label are printed on FSC® certified paper. FSC is the only forest certification scheme
endorsed by the leading environmental organisations, including Greenpeace. Our paper
procurement policy can be found at www.randomhouse.co.uk/environment

Typeset by Palimpsest Book Production Limited,
Falkirk, Stirlingshire

Printed and bound by CPI Group
(UK) Ltd, Croydon, CR0 4YY

This book is dedicated to Evelyn Makasi and to the futures of all the children at the Abaphumeleli Home of Safety in the heart of the Khayelitsha Township in South Africa.

www.albertjack.com/brighterfuture

CONTENTS

INTRODUCTION

'A special kind of beauty exists which is born in language, of language, and for language' – Gaston Bachelard

'The finest language is mostly made up of simple unimposing words' – George Eliot

The English language is perhaps the richest and most expressive in the world. One of the reasons for this is that we have so many weird and wonderful ways of describing exactly the same thing: we can be as colourful or as plain with our language as we choose.

This is what has brought me to *It's a Wonderful Word*. On the face of it the history of the English language is, at best, rather dull. Over the centuries words inspired by invaders or enemies or trading partners have attached themselves to the nebulous thing known as the English language, but that really is pretty much it. It is certainly not easy to write an entertaining book on the subject – or so I thought. When I looked a little closer – and in a slightly different way from that of etymologists and scholars with minds far greater than mine – I discovered all sorts of fascinating tales.

Because, alongside the usual Latin-based words we picked up from the Romans and the words nicked from the Celts and Picts and other ancient Europeans, the English language has drawn its inspiration from some exceedingly odd places: clowns, facial hair, items of furniture, famous elephants . . . you name it. So in these pages I hope to PANDER to your curiosity thanks to a historical pimp, MESMERISE you thanks to hypnotist Dr Franz Mesmer, and leave you GOOGLY-EYED with amazement thanks to an American cartoon strip.

And then there are the words that look and sound as if someone just plucked them out of thin air: SKULDUGGERY, CODSWALLOP, JIGGERY-POKERY, CLAPTRAP. But rest assured these words are not mere GOBBLEDYGOOK: there's a cracking story behind each one.

As my research progressed I found myself ever more fascinated by English-speaking people and our shared English-speaking history. There is so much about our cultures that can be learned through the strange journeys our words have made: how the medieval SHERIFF ended up in the Wild West; how an African snake-god inspired Hollywood's ZOMBIES; how an English queen was defeated by Irish

BLARNEY and a Scottish queen by Portuguese MARMALADE; and how words from POMMY to BARRACKING have got lost in translation en route to Australia.

Some distinct themes emerged as I delved into the backgrounds of our favourite words. Amid the genteel romance of the eighteenth and nineteenth centuries I found out what playing GOOSEBERRY has to do with gooseberries and what CANOODLING has to do with canoes. As I approached the twentieth century I came across an increasing number of words to describe drunkenness, from ADDLED and SOZZLED to BLOTTO and BEFUDDLED, via MULLERED, PIE-EYED and BINGEING.

But by far the most popular and most wonderful of English words come from the noble art of insulting people. Whether you call someone an IGNORAMUS, a NINCOMPOOP, a PIPSQUEAK, a BUMPKIN, a JACKANAPES, a SCALLYWAG or a PIKEY, you are keeping alive a word that has travelled across borders and through centuries to get here, and surely nobody could take offence at that.

I hope you enjoy exploring this ode to the English language as much as I have enjoyed writing it. It turns out etymology is one of the most exciting –ologies out there.

Albert Jack
Guildford, 2011

NAMES AND PLACES

Technically, the first person ever to **mesmerise** anyone – that is, to leave someone spellbound at what they have seen or heard – was Dr Franz Anton Mesmer (1734–1815), a leading Austrian physician who ruffled a few feathers in the medical establishment by using hypnotism as a way of treating illness. It was his belief that ill health was caused by obstructions in the harmonious ebb and flow of magnetic fluid circulating the body, and his treatment involved putting the patient into a trance-like state and then passing a magnet over the skin in order to free the blockage. This not only marked the birth of hypnotism but also paved the way for attempts at paranormal communication, which soon attracted its own devotees.

That said, the medical profession remained sceptical about Mesmer's unconventional beliefs, and it took the dedication of his later followers for them to be accorded their own special term: **mesmerism**. The word was current by 1829 and the associated 'mesmerised' was used to describe anybody in a trance-like state, chemically assisted or otherwise. In 1841, Scottish surgeon James Braid (1795–1860) used the principles of mesmerism for a series of lectures on the subject of hypnotherapy that eventually established his own reputation as the father of modern hypnosis.

Maverick, a word famously beloved of Sarah Palin, is generally used to describe an innovative, independent-minded individual. Perhaps ironically, all of these supposedly independent-minded individuals are aping the characteristics of a single historical figure, Samuel A. Maverick (1803–70). Maverick was a Texas cattle rancher who caused a bit of a stir by leaving his cattle unbranded, something no other rancher had dared to do, for fear of rustlers. Unusually for a man of his period and occupation, Maverick had realised that branding animals was exceptionally cruel, but he had also realised that leaving them unbranded meant he could claim any unbranded animal as his own: the more conventional ranchers would have to agree that they must be his. Maverick became so well known that, by the time of his death, his name was being used to describe politicians who refused to affiliate themselves with a particular cause, and the expression has widened in its application ever since. (See also GOBBLEDYGOOK.)

A **silhouette** is a shadow profile, usually of a person, cut out of black paper and depicting only the outline of the sitter's head. The popularity of silhouettes grew during the eighteenth century, particularly in France, as an inexpensive form of portrait for those who could not afford anything more lavish. Basically, they were the poor man's painting.

Silhouettes are named after one Etienne de Silhouette (1709–67), a French politician during the reign of Louis XV. In March 1759, Silhouette was given the position of Controller-General, with special responsibility for strengthening the nation's finances during the Seven Years' War (1756–63) with Britain and other nations. To this end, he introduced a method of taxing the rich, although he was careful not to include either the nobility or the church, all of which made him incredibly unpopular in most quarters of French society. His blatant favouritism of the king's court helped fuel the popular outrage that ultimately led to the Storming of the Bastille in July 1789 and the subsequent French Revolution (1789–99), in which Louis XVI and thousands of his supporters from the privileged classes were executed (see GUILLOTINE). Meanwhile, his austere tax reforms earned him a lasting association with all things cheap, with the term *à la Silhouette* being applied to them, including the inexpensive cut-out portraits that were all the rage at the time.

None of us like to feel we have been cheated or **diddled** out of something that belongs to us, do we? Although the word looks as if it might have evolved from two others that mean much the same – 'do' and FIDDLE – it does in fact come from the name of a person, the notorious but fictional conman Jeremy Diddler. Diddler was the creation of James Kenney (1780–1849), a prolific playwright who produced more than forty stage dramas and operas. It was his first play, a farce called *Raising the Wind* (1803), that introduced the character to the public. Diddler's preferred way of 'raising the wind' – an expression for getting hold of cash in any way possible – was to continually borrow small sums without ever paying anybody back, better known nowadays as sponging. The play and the character were so popular that 'diddle', based on the character's name, passed into standard English as a way of describing the type of swindling he was associated with. (See also ROOKIE.)

Gypsies used to have a rather romantic reputation as nomads from far, far away, who were just passing through on their way to exciting new lands. They must have made quite an impression when they turned up in the remote villages of England during the sixteenth century. But although they travelled stealthily, they would not have been able to get much further than Wales, which must have rather ruined their mystique. By contrast, the image of the modern-day Gypsy is rather less idealised – no thanks to various instructive reality TV shows – and more likely to be associated with scrap-metal yards, pub brawls and house breaking.

Gypsies were originally so named, back in the sixteenth century, because it was assumed that they had travelled from Egypt. Many had indeed come to Europe via Egypt, although they had originally set off from Southeast Asia. Their 'open road' lifestyle was for a long time envied by many. The nineteenth-century travel writer George Borrow, for instance, wrote in his introduction to *The Zincali; or, An Account of the Gypsies of Spain* (1841): 'Throughout my life the Gypsy race has always had a peculiar interest for me. Indeed I can remember no period when the mere mention of the name of Gypsy did not awaken within me feelings hard to be described.' A sentiment that I imagine is shared today among members of the British farming community, although I expect the feelings awakened within them are somewhat different and perhaps best not described.

George Borrow also introduced the term **Romany**, to denote European Gypsies, in his semi-autobiographical novel *The Romany Rye* of 1857. The book dealt with his time travelling with the Romany people, who had been migrating across Europe since the eleventh century. Due to their itinerant lifestyle, they weren't always welcomed but regarded with suspicion, often accused of thieving. In 1530, Henry VIII signed the Egyptians Act into law, which gave the Gypsies sixteen days to leave the country, during which they were to restore any stolen goods to their rightful owners. His daughter Queen Mary (the one NICKNAMED Bloody Mary because of all the Protestants she had burned at the stake) amended the act in 1554, adding even stricter punishments for anyone pursuing a Gypsy lifestyle but allowing any Gypsy 'that shall honestly exercise himself in some lawful Work or Occupation' to stay. The following decade, another law allowed those born in England to stay put, too. Thanks to these loopholes, the Gypsies found it slightly easier to evade deportation and began to settle in the country.

In France the Gypsy travellers were called *bohémiens*, because they were thought – incorrectly – to have come from the Kingdom of Bohemia in what is now the Czech Republic. The word **bohemian** subsequently entered the English language as a way of describing anyone artistic and unconventional, as William Makepeace Thackeray depicts his heroine in *Vanity Fair* (1848): '[Becky Sharp] was of a wild, roving nature, inherited from father and mother, who were both Bohemians, by taste and circumstance.' (See also PIKEY, POSH.)

To be in **limbo** is to be caught between two extremes, usually metaphorical, although in Christian theology Limbo is a place on the borders of Hell, home to the souls of unbaptised infants and upstanding adults who had died before the resurrection of Christ and hence before he could open the gates of Heaven to let them in. The word comes from the Latin *limbus*, 'edge' or 'border'.

Medieval theologians defined Limbo as two of the four distinct parts of the underworld. The first two, the Hell of the Damned and Purgatory, were reserved for the wicked and the evil. In the Hell of the Damned, souls would be punished for ever. Purgatory was slightly less severe: the souls of the wicked and evil who had repented during their lifetime would go there to be punished, but only for a while. On the edges of Hell were the other two, the Limbo of the Fathers and the Limbo of the Infants. The first was reserved for the good souls who were waiting for the gates of Heaven to open, while the second was reserved for infants who had not been baptised or who were too young to be responsible for any wicked actions.

Neither kind of Limbo has anything to do with the Caribbean art of **limbo dancing** – in which the dancer bends backwards to pass under a pole that is progressively lowered – that came to public attention during the West Indian migration to Britain in the 1950s. The word is related to the word 'limber', as in 'supple', said to derive from a dialect word of the sixteenth century for a cart shaft, perhaps in allusion to its to-and-fro movement when pulled by a horse. Limbo dances are based on the types of dance that were traditionally performed at funerals among African communities, to symbolise the triumph of life over death – as represented by the bent-over dancer emerging victoriously from beneath the lowered pole.

To be doing something all on your **tod** means you are completely alone with no help or assistance from anybody else. Its background is COCKNEY rhyming slang based on the story of a man who began his life alone and ended it in much the same way.

James Forman 'Tod' Sloan was born in 1874 in Indiana.

His mother died when he was only five years old and his father soon sent him to live with another family. A solitary child, Tod took on work at the nearby oil fields but soon found employment at a stable in St Louis, where he lived among the horses. By the time he was eleven, he had moved to Kansas City and was working as a stable lad for a racehorse trainer. This was the turning point in young Tod's life: within ten years, he had become a jockey and was riding in races on the East Coast, where he dominated the scene by showcasing his famous 'monkey man' crouching style, since used by most professional jockeys. Thanks to his incredible success – he won nearly half of all the races he entered – he was brought to England in 1901 and installed as the Prince of Wales' senior jockey. The loner from Indiana was now surrounded by the rich, the famous, the great and the good, travelling everywhere with his own personal valet.

But the good times were not to last. Despite or perhaps because of his spectacular success, the grandees of the British Jockey Club resented the young American and his larger-than-life personality, and they persuaded the prince not to renew Sloan's racing contract. His licence was revoked for unspecified reasons, although the rumour was that he had illegally been betting on races he was competing in. Sloan was all but ostracised by the racing communities on both sides of the Atlantic, and, although he managed to use some of his wealth to convert a small bistro in Paris into what is now Harry's New York Bar, financial problems forced him back to America, where he lived out the remainder of his life alone and in debt, dying of cirrhosis of the liver in 1933.

But his fame was secured and the mark he made on the racing scene has never really diminished. George M. Cohan's endearing song 'The Yankee Doodle Boy' was based on Tod Sloan's sad life in England. Londoners subsequently awarded the jockey the highest accolade imaginable: a place in the lexicon of Cockney rhyming slang. To be **all on your tod** is to be 'alone like Tod Sloan'. Even his autobiography, published in 1915, was poignantly entitled *Tod Sloan by Himself*.

It was the French Revolution that made a certain Dr Joseph-Ignace Guillotin (1738–1814) world famous, although ironically he did not invent the machine that caused nearly 40,000 French heads to roll. Originally known as a *louisette* after the name of its creator, the **guillotine** was actually invented by a military surgeon called Antoine Louis; Guillotin himself was publicly opposed to capital punishment.

In 1784, when Franz Mesmer (see MESMERISED) published his theory of animal magnetism, the French public were so offended by his conclusions that Louis XVI established a commission to investigate the matter, which included Dr Guillotin, by then an eminent physician. In 1789, following publication the previous year of his pamphlet *Petition of the Citizens Living in Paris*, Guillotin was appointed one of the ten Paris Deputies of the Assemblée Constituante. During a debate on capital punishment, he proposed that 'the criminal should be decapitated and solely by means of a simple mechanism, a machine that beheads painlessly'. It was Guillotin's belief that, if an execution had to be carried out, it should at least be pain-free. His initiative led to proposals for a new 'death machine', and the development of the *louisette*, later renamed the 'guillotine'.

There is a common misconception that Guillotin was himself eventually executed by the machine that bore his name, but, although he was arrested and imprisoned for a short time, he was released in 1794. The Dr J. M.V. Guillotin who was dispatched at Lyon during the early 1790s was a different person altogether. Our Dr Guillotin retired from politics and returned to the safety of the medical profession, becoming one of the founders of the Academy of Medicine in Paris. Guillotin was also one of the most vocal supporters of Edward Jenner's theory of vaccination, which has saved millions of lives over the last two centuries.

After Guillotin's death, of natural causes, in 1814, his family, embarrassed by the infamous death machine, petitioned the French government to change its name. When their appeal was turned down, they changed theirs instead, and have lived in peaceful obscurity ever since.

Anywhere described as **Bedlam** is guaranteed to be a place of uncontrolled chaos, which is precisely the opposite of what the benevolent people behind the word had in mind.

In 1547, Henry VIII gave the City of London the Priory of St Mary of Bethlehem in Bishopsgate, which had been established 300 years earlier, for use as a hospital. Bethlem, as it was known, was designed to house the mentally unstable.

When the asylum was later transferred to Moorfields, it became a popular tourist attraction. Incredibly, the governors charged admission for tickets, allowing the public to witness the bizarre behaviour of the inmates and in many cases even encouraged visitors to goad them on. It's absurd to think that anyone in their right mind could actually be entertained by a bunch of poor deluded people in a compromised state of dignity. Oh, hang on. That sounds like *The X Factor* and *Big Brother* to me.

Over time, 'Bethlem' became 'Bedlam' and the word associated with scenes of human degradation. In 1800, the asylum moved again to Lambeth and again in 1930 to Aldington in Surrey. Today it is known as the Bethlem Royal Hospital and is located in Beckenham in Kent.

Although some people mistakenly assume the world's most popular ballpoint pen to be the creation of American cartoonist and comic book publisher Charles **Biro** (1911–72), the real inventor of the famous writing implement was in fact Hungarian journalist László József Bíró (1899–1985). He noticed how quickly newspaper ink dried during the printing process and decided to experiment with it in his fountain pen. The ink proved too sticky to flow properly but it had given him the idea for a practical, quick-drying pen, which he and his chemist brother Georg eventually patented in 1938. After the Second World War, an expert in writing implements named Marcel Bich bought Bíró's patent for the ballpoint pen, adding the Bic Biro to his growing portfolio of disposable products, which also includes the Bic Lighter and Bic Razor.

To stage a **boycott** is to withdraw from a commercial or social commitment in protest or as a punishment, and is yet another interesting word that has entered the language from Ireland (see BANSHEE for references to many more).

In the 1870s, Captain Charles Cunningham Boycott, an Englishman, was working as a land agent for the powerful landowner Lord Erne at Loughmask in County Mayo. In September 1880, a campaign organised by the Irish Land League called for a reform of the system of landholding; protesting tenants demanded that Captain Boycott initiate a substantial discount in their rent payments. It was a sensitive time, given that 30 per cent of the country's men had already left for either England, where they worked as NAVVIES, or for the New World, from which they rarely returned. Labour resources were therefore very thin on the ground. Even so, Boycott refused to submit to the demands of the Irish Land League, even ordering anyone with rent arrears to be evicted. Charles Parnell, the president of the Land League, made a speech calling for everybody in the local community – not just Boycott's tenants – to refuse to have anything to do with the unpopular agent, in support of their own cause.

The result was that labourers refused to work for him, shop- and innkeepers declined to serve either him or his family, and even the postal staff stopped delivering his letters. Boycott had to go to the expense of having his own food brought in, under guard, from great distances away; fifty labourers were brought all the way from Ulster to save the harvest on his lands, the workers protected by an armed guard of 900 men. The whole affair had been an expensive mistake for Boycott, but an incredible success for the tenants. It roused so much passion and attention, even over in London, that the Land League called upon all Irishmen and women to oppose similar landlords or their agents as they had opposed Boycott. Within weeks, 'boycott', in the sense of 'refusal to cooperate', had been adopted by newspapers around Europe, and subsequently the world. By the time the captain died in 1897, having fled back to England at the end of 1880, his name had become an accepted part of the English language.

Doolally describes a person who has 'lost his marbles' or 'gone round the bend'. It is an anglicised version of Deolali, the name of a hill station 100 miles northeast of Bombay, where there was a British army base during the nineteenth century. Deolali served mainly as a transition camp at which soldiers would be stationed before travelling back to Britain at the end of their tours of duty, but it also housed an asylum where battle-weary and unstable troops could be treated before making the long journey home. Since the transport ships sailed only between November and March, so as to avoid dangerous bad weather, some soldiers had to wait for many months at Deolali. Heat exhaustion coupled with complete boredom often led to strange, eccentric behaviour, which the troops NICKNAMED 'Deolali tap', *tap* being the Urdu word for 'fever'. Back in England, anybody who had 'gone through Deolali' was assumed to have lost his mind.

This unassuming Indian town also inspired another slang term for much the same thing. In 1919, the Surgeon General of the US army was quoted denying that 'there is any foundation for the stories being circulated of the existence of **basket cases** in our hospitals'. He was talking about the existence (or otherwise) of returning soldiers who were suffering from shell shock or other mental illness. At that time, basket weaving was a common activity in both American and British military hospitals, having been introduced at Deolali in an attempt to find simple but time-consuming activities to help the men while away the long wait.

On a lighter note, the Royal Artillery Depot at Deolali was the setting for the first four series of the popular 1970s British sitcom *It Ain't Half Hot Mum*.

'**Kilroy** was here.' Much has been speculated and written about the mythical Kilroy and why he seemed to be everywhere, including my school pencil case, during the second half of the twentieth century.

The idea behind the Kilroy phenomenon was that he could turn up anywhere in the world – but only in the most unusual and unlikely places. I wouldn't be surprised to find his name etched into the dust on the moon. The phrase 'Kilroy was here' originated in America, where it was regarded as something of a national craze and was often accompanied by a cartoon of a little man with a big nose peeking over a wall. It was so popular by the time of the Second World War that Russian psychopath Joseph Stalin, returning from the VIP bathroom during the Potsdam Conference in 1945, had to ask his aides who this Kilroy was. Captured German intelligence later revealed that the name was spotted so frequently on American military equipment that the other great psychopath of the era, Adolf Hitler, believed it to be a codeword and became paranoid in his attempts to find out what it meant.

The real Kilroy was revealed in 1946 by the *New York Times* to have been James J. Kilroy, a shipyard inspector who was based at the Fore River Shipyard in Quincy, Massachusetts, during the Second World War. He was identified after a national competition was run by the Amalgamated Transit Union in an attempt to unravel the mystery. Kilroy himself then explained how the phrase had arisen. According to him, the wages of riveters were based on the number of rivets fitted during a shift and each man would mark his last rivet so his pay could be calculated by the shipyard inspector. If the next shift started before the inspector had made his calculations, however, the men had been known to move the chalk markings back many dozens of rivets in order to make their output appear far greater than it really was. Kilroy put a stop to this by drawing a line beneath the final rivet of a particular shift and writing 'Kilroy was here', so that the next worker would know the area had already been inspected.

And that is how 'Kilroy' began turning up in the most unusual locations on board a ship: sealed inside the hull, upside down beneath the bridge, down near the waterline, and in numerous other seemingly inaccessible places. Tens of thousands of servicemen encountered the strange Kilroy, sparking the legend that he was actually a protective spirit. In September 1946, a singer called Paul Page released a novelty song called 'Kilroy Was Here', which helped the phrase go global by the end of that decade.

Bakelite was one of the first ever man-made materials, and the forefather of just about every piece of plastic you may have around you. It was developed in 1909 by Belgian chemist Leo Baekeland (1863–1944), after whom it was named; early mass-produced radios, telephones and electrical insulators were all Bakelite products. It had become a staple material in all areas of manufacture and industry by the 1920s and was a major influence on the development of modern synthetics.

Aborigines are thought to have arrived in the land we now call Australia up to 125,000 years ago, although the first evidence of human remains only dates back a mere 40,000 years. Either way, the people weren't called Aborigines then, and the land down under wasn't known as Australia. It wasn't until 1606, in fact, that the continent received its current name: Dutch explorers recorded a landmass in the Southern Hemisphere and named it 'Australis', which means 'southern' in Latin, a reference to the imagined *Terra Australis Incognita*, 'unknown land of the south', that appeared on European maps from the fifteenth to the eighteenth century. It was the English who actually claimed the land, in 1770, following Captain James Cook's legendary first voyage to the continent, during which he encountered the indigenous people for the first time.

As the eighteenth century drew to a close, the British began transporting prisoners and other undesirables to their new territory and it was the British colonists who, from 1820, began to call the native people **aboriginal**, the word borrowed from the Latin *aborigine*, 'from the beginning', from which 'original' also derives. In Roman mythology, the Aborigines were the oldest or 'original' inhabitants of central Italy, believed to have come down from the mountains and occupied the town of Latium, the former capital of the Roman Empire.

To **josh** somebody is to tease them or lead them on in a harmless way. There is a great story connected with this word, concerning a deaf mute named Josh Tatum, who, in 1883, began gold-plating nickel coins and was able to pass them off as solid gold five-dollar pieces (see also BUCK). Tatum realised that every time he used one of these bogus coins to buy something worth five cents, he would be given $4.95 in change, and in no time amassed a small fortune. These 'racketeer nickels', as they became known, were soon withdrawn from circulation, but not before Josh found himself up before the judge. Tatum's defence successfully argued that, since he could neither hear nor speak, he hadn't passed the nickel off as a five-dollar coin and hadn't asked for change: he had simply accepted what the shopkeeper gave him and left. The case against him was quickly dropped.

Many of the racketeer nickels of 1883 remain in private collections to this day and sometimes come up at coin fairs and festivals. You could pick one up for around $25, a nice reminder of the day the deaf mute conman stopped the US Mint in its tracks and gave his name to the gentle art of teasing. Which is a fantastic tale, and widely believed, but sadly isn't true. Indeed, there is no indication, other than in connection with this story, that Josh Tatum ever lived. Of the four Josh Tatums recorded on the 1880 US Federal Census none of them were deaf mutes.

But the name 'Josh' may well have given rise to the word. Earlier in the nineteenth century, 'Josh' (as a diminutive of 'Joshua') was, according to the *Random House Historic Dictionary of American Slang*, a typically rural name associated with a BUMPKIN or HICK. The *Oxford English Dictionary*, meanwhile, suggests a connection with the well-known humorist Henry Wheeler Shaw (1818–85), who between 1860 and 1880 gave popular lectures of his writings under the pseudonym 'Josh Billings'. On top of all this, there is the small matter of an edition of the *St Louis Reveille* newspaper in 1845 which provides the earliest example of the word in print: 'Look out in future, and if you must josh, do it privately.' All of which appears once and for all to relieve coin trickster Josh Tatum of his notoriety.

To call a man a **guy** is a common enough thing to do, especially in America. But why 'guy'? The answer is as surprising as it is obvious. On 5 November 1605 in cold dark London town, a chap called Guido Fawkes, otherwise known as Guy, was discovered trying to plant twenty barrels of gunpowder in the cellars of the Houses of Parliament, in an attempt to blow the place – and the king – to pieces.

Four hundred years later, many of us may argue that Guy Fawkes was the last person ever to enter that building with honest intentions, but the authorities at the time were not amused. Fawkes and his co-conspirators in the Gunpowder Plot were dispatched in a most gruesome and medieval manner, as a warning to other like-minded Catholics. To prevent Guy Fawkes from becoming a national hero or martyr, King James I commanded that the date of the failed plot be commemorated with public fires and patriotic festivities. Since then, the remit of 'Bonfire Night' has been expanded to include fireworks and the burning of Guy Fawkes effigies, which are historically paraded through town before being tossed on to a fire. By the nineteenth century, these effigies were simply known as 'guys' – although some towns have replaced their 'guys' with 'tonies', thanks to a more recent popular enemy.

While 5 November means little to the average American, the word 'guy' to denote any nameless male (or sometimes female) is very much rooted in the anti-terrorist celebrations of their seventeenth-century forebears.

Albion, the ancient (and rather romantic) name for Britain, is generally believed to be related to the Latin *albus*, 'white', in reference to the iconic cliffs at Dover, which have historically been the first view of the country for any foreign traveller, including the Romans.

But there is also a myth about the giant son of Neptune, Roman god of the sea, who was called Albion and who was said to have discovered the British Isles and ruled over them for forty-four years. An unrelated tale, meanwhile, involves the fifty daughters of the King of Syria, who all married on the same day and marked the occasion by murdering their husbands on the wedding night. As punishment they were set adrift in a ship and finally ran ashore on the coast of what we now call Britain. Here the daughters, the eldest of whom was called Albia, established a colony, married the locals and formed their own new civilisation of Albions.

In 1579, the great explorer Sir Francis Drake annexed an area of land in what is now called California and claimed it for his queen, Elizabeth I. A plaque marking this discovery referred to the territory as New Albion.

A **Machiavellian** politician or businessman is known to be unscrupulous and deceitful, taking risks at other people's expense. An oft-quoted early example of Machiavellianism in action is the St Bartholomew's Day Massacre of 1572, a series of political assassinations in Paris followed by rioting and violence at the hands of Roman Catholic mobs, popularly thought to have been ordered by Catherine de Medici as a way of ridding the largely Catholic city of prominent Huguenot Protestants.

The word 'Machievel' was well enough known in England just twenty years later to have been used by the playwright Christopher Marlowe as the name of a minor character in his *Jew of Malta*. Shakespeare likewise used the word in *The Merry Wives of Windsor* in 1602: 'Am I politic? Am I subtle?

Am I a Machiavel?' Marlowe's final play, *The Massacre at Paris* (1593), portrays Catherine de Medici and her crony the Duke of Guise as inherently evil tyrants – or what we would nowadays call 'Machiavellian'. But what is all of this a reference to?

Niccolò Machiavelli (1469–1527) was an Italian diplomat, writer and philosopher who is considered to be one of the founders of modern political thought. His best-known book, *The Prince*, published in 1532, became the blueprint for Tudor and Elizabethan politics. Its central message is that only a strong and ruthless ruler can free a country from occupation and devastation by foreigners, and that tyranny and deceit are justified if they secure peace and prosperity for a nation. His ideas were simplified and exaggerated by the power-hungry monarchs and politicians who read them, and Machiavelli's name became a byword for viciousness and cunning on an epic scale.

FOOD AND DRINK

At the end of the eighteenth century, word of a new French fashion crossed the English Channel. Apparently the French were enjoying a new type of informal party known as a *pique-nique*, to which the guests brought along a share of the food and wine so that the burden of providing would not be left to only one family. Never ones to let the French get the upper hand, the British began holding **picnics** in outdoor public places.

The word *pique* means 'to pick' and *nique* once translated into English as 'of no importance'. (It now has an entirely different slang meaning that I couldn't possibly print here.) According to the *Oxford English Dictionary*, the word 'picnic' was first used in English during the mid–eighteenth century in association with poker playing, but it gradually came to describe a meal of many small cold dishes eaten during a hunt, a tradition dating back to the mid-fourteenth century and usually involving game pies and roasted or baked meats.

When the great royal parks of Paris were opened to the public following the French Revolution, *pique-nique* culture took off with a vengeance and Londoners who were used to looking to Paris for the latest fashions promptly set up their own version, the 'Picnic Society', whose members would each arrive with their share of the overall feast. The nationwide enjoyment of picnicking rocketed during the nineteenth century, helped along by popular fictionalisations of informal outdoor feasts by the likes of Jane Austen and Charles Dickens.

A **bistro** is the sort of fast-food café people visited before American ultra-fast-food outlets began to take over our high streets in the 1970s. After the defeat of Napoleon at the Battle of Waterloo in 1815, troops from all over Europe began to occupy Paris, particularly the Russians. Naturally the French cafés were soon bustling with new visitors and trade was roaring, and one of the most frequent shouts to be heard at the time was '*Bystro! Bystro!*', which means 'Quickly! Quickly!' in Russian. Hence the word soon became associated with cheap bars, small clubs and cafés.

Any fan of Jamie Oliver will know that **pukka** is probably the most overused word in the whole kingdom of Essex. Perhaps surprisingly, it does actually have a culinary association.

25

The term originally came to prominence at the height of the British Raj (see BUNGALOW) as part of the expression *pukka sahib*, 'real gentleman' or 'splendid chap'. It derives from the Hindi word *pakka* meaning 'properly cooked' or 'substantial' and hence came to be used to describe anything that is approved of or deemed genuine (see also KOSHER). So when Jamie next serves up a steaming dish and describes it as 'pukka', it could well mean that he knows he is giving a nod to the field kitchens of the British Empire. But I somehow doubt it, don't you?

Avocado is a pear-shaped fruit, sometimes called the 'alligator pear', which is native to the state of Puebla in Mexico. The Spanish name for the fruit, *aguacate*, comes from the native Nahuatl word *ahuácatl*, which means 'testicles' (see also BOLLOCKS, KNACKER), in reference to the shape of the fruit. Hang on, I have one in my fridge: I shall go and check. OK, I can see their point. I wonder what the first South American dock workers must have imagined as they loaded crates stamped with the local word for 'testicles' on to ships bound for Europe.

Incidentally, the word **orchid** is taken directly from the Greek word *orkhis*, which also means 'testicle', thanks, apparently, to the shape of the flower's root. But as I don't have any orchids lying around here, we shall have to take their word for it this time. 'Orchid', you may be interested to know, was introduced to the English language by the eminent botanist John Lindley in his book *School Botany* (1845).

The meaning of the word **sandwich** has absolutely nothing to do with bread, ham or Cheddar, but it famously has a connection with an earl. When Charles II's naval commander Sir Edward Montague was made an earl in gratitude for his loyal service to the king, he was given a choice of great ports after which to name himself. He settled eventually for Sandwich, a bustling seaport in its day but now just a quaint town in Kent, whose name in Old English meant 'Sand Village'.

It was not Edward Montague but his great-grandson, John, the 4th earl (1718–92), who provided the crucial element of every packed lunch in the Western world, and all thanks to his dissolute nature. Having followed his ancestor's footsteps and ended up First Lord of the Admiralty, Sandwich turned the navy into a chaotically mismanaged organisation; the defeat of the British forces in the American War of Independence (1775–83) was seen by many as his fault. The earl was far more interested in his life outside work, particularly gambling, and legend has it that he was at the card table when he inadvertently invented the world's most versatile snack.

It was 1762 and Sandwich was gambling with friends. Drunk and enjoying a run of good luck, he ordered the servants to bring him meat, but between two slices of bread so that the grease wouldn't get onto his fingers and mark the cards. This unusual request proved a success and the so-called 'sandwich' soon caught on at other gaming tables before becoming an integral part of English cuisine.

Sadly this revolutionary culinary invention did nothing for Sandwich's terrible reputation, and by the time of his death he had become one of the most unpopular men in England. He famously fell victim to one of history's great putdowns at a meeting of the notorious Hellfire Club, a satirical and very secretive gentlemen's club set up to ridicule organised religion, after he had abused dramatist Samuel Foote by declaring, 'Sir, I don't know if you will die on the gallows or of the pox.' Quick as a flash, Foote shot back: 'That, sir, depends on whether I embrace your principles or your mistress.'

Remarkably, considering Sandwich's dubious talents, the sandwich is not his only legacy to history. As First Lord of the Admiralty he was one of the sponsors of Captain Cook's voyage to the New World in 1788, and when Cook discovered the Hawaiian Islands he called them the Sandwich Lands in honour of his benefactor. Although the islands changed names a century later, the South Sandwich Islands and the Sandwich Straits still bear the old rogue's name. Had he chosen one of the more famous ports as his title, I could have been eating a tuna and sweetcorn portsmouth today, or a cheese and chutney dover.

Slap-bang in the middle is right at the centre of something, not a word you might associate with food, you might think, but this is where the expression began life originally. The rise of the working and middle classes following the Reform Act of 1832 – which greatly increased the size of the electorate, giving many more people the vote – led to a sharp increase in cheaper amenities on the streets of British cities, of which 'slap-bang' eating houses were an integral part. Charles Dickens mentioned this new social dining scene in his 1839 story 'Making a Night of It', from *Sketches*

by Boz: 'They lived in the same street, walked into town every morning at the same hour, dined at the same slap-bang every day.' These cheap eateries became known as slap-bangs because a patron would 'slap' his money down on the table and a plate of prepared food would be 'banged' down right in front of him. It's thought that they are also behind the expression **slap-up**, to describe a different kind of eating experience – a great meal in a POSH restaurant. (See also SLAPDASH.)

The most popular story behind the word **marmalade** is that it derives from *Marie malade* ('ill Mary' in French), referring to Mary, Queen of Scots, supposedly using it to settle her stomach during a bout of terrible seasickness in the mid-sixteenth century. This is certainly the derivation that respected etymologist Michael Caine (yes, *that* Michael Caine) once revealed during a television interview, so surely it must be correct.

Actually: probably not. The word was in fact being used quite a few years before Mary's time: possibly as early as 1480, according to the *Oxford English Dictionary*. It is easy to see how the seasick queen got involved, though: in French, the word *mer* means 'sea' and *malade* means 'sick'. But long before Mary was vomiting her state banquet into the English Channel, *marmelada* was the Portuguese name for a sweet quince paste ('quince' is *marmelo* in that language), which was imported as a luxury to Britain from the late fifteenth century onwards. So expensive that it was used only by royalty and the well heeled, *marmelada* was nonetheless in great demand. Tudor cooks invented a more affordable version by boiling up cheaper imports, such as lemons and bitter Seville oranges, into thick, solid conserves they called 'marmalades', which were then cut into slices and eaten as sweets – similar in consistency to Turkish delight.

Small enough to be bite-sized, **canapés** are served either hot or cold and can be held in one hand, while, most importantly, the drinking hand remains accessible at all times. Generally served as a snack, appetiser or starter, traditional canapés are little platforms of pastry, toast or crackers with any variety of more interesting foods sitting upon them, which makes the literal translation of this French word – 'couch' or 'settee' – quite apt.

Hors d'oeuvres, pronounced 'ordurves' on this side of the Channel, are a grown-up version of canapés. They are essentially the same thing but are slightly larger, requiring two bites, and with more imaginative toppings such as sardines, smoked fish, caviar or olives. Hors d'oeuvres became a familiar feature in restaurants all over Europe at the turn of the twentieth century, the expression having evolved in the kitchens of the great chefs of Paris a century earlier. Literally translated, *hors* means 'outside' in French, and *oeuvre* means 'work' (as in 'masterpiece'): in other words, the hors d'oeuvres are the warm-up band for the headlining act.

31

The splendidly named **wayzgoose** was once the traditional annual feast provided by a master printer for his workers around St Bartholomew's Day, 24 August. It marked the end of the summer months in England and ushered in the season of working by candlelight over the long winter months. Over time, the wayzgoose evolved into an annual day-long outing that major employers provided for their workers and families, especially once the development of the railway network made visits to the seaside possible. Some of the larger companies of the industrial age even commissioned entire trains or took over several hotels for what was to be the event of the year.

'Wayz' is a now obsolete English word for a bundle of hay or straw, which signified the harvest and hence the end of the summer. For the second half of the word we need to consider what those employees would have eaten at a wayzgoose, in earlier times at least. Until the **turkey** took over as the festive bird of choice in the later nineteenth century – it is indeed named after the country, incidentally, despite being native to America, because it resembles the turkeycock, now confusingly called guineafowl, that was imported from Asia via Turkey (still with me?) – the goose was the favoured bird. So the traditional fare for a wayzgoose would have been, well, a wayzgoose: a harvest goose. Even when the goose ceased to be the centrepiece of the event, the great annual outing followed tradition and continued to be named after it. (See also BEANFEAST, SHINDIG.)

Ah, **mayonnaise**. The versatile white sauce, found in refrigerators all over the world, is a simple mix of olive oil with lemon juice and egg yolk. The classic French food encyclopaedia *Larousse Gastronomique* asserts that 'Mayonnaise, in our view, is a popular corruption of *moyeunaise*, derived from the old French word *moyeu*, meaning "egg yolk".' A second possible French connection is to Charles de Lorraine, Duke of Mayenne, because he once, according to legend, took so long eating a meal of chicken with white sauce that he lost the Battle of Arques in 1589. (Actually, he seems to have lost that battle in the traditional French fashion: running away after being confronted by 4,000 British reinforcements.)

Then there are vague reports of a certain Irish army general called MacMahon, who claimed to have invented the sauce, while the deluded-sounding inhabitants of the French city of Bayonne are convinced it was originally called *Bayonnaise*.

More likely than all of these is that mayonnaise as we know it today is named after Port Mahon, capital of Menorca. After the French, led by the Duke of Richelieu, liberated the British-occupied city in 1756, they took the recipe for the popular Spanish condiment aioli back to France with them, controversially omitted the garlic, and called the new creation *Mahonnaise*, in honour of their great victory over the British. It has been a regular addition to British food since the 1840s.

A **beanfeast** is much the same sort of affair as a WAYZGOOSE: an annual celebration of Christmas or a company anniversary that is meant to promote harmony and goodwill among employees but will often degenerate into drunken brawls and illicit encounters behind the photocopier. In these days of political correctness, such outings are better known as 'bonding' or 'team-building' exercises, but originally they were recognised for what they actually were: a good old knees-up (see also SHINDIG).

There are two suggestions as to how we began using the word 'beanfeast'. The first relates to the bean goose, which generally descends on Britain in the autumn and has bean-shaped markings on its bill. In the nineteenth century, the bird was readily available and relatively cheap, and therefore served to employees by Scrooge-like bosses – hence 'beanfeast'. The second suggestion is that the phrase has its roots in the 'beans and bacon' traditionally served at such parties. 'Beanfeast' has in turn led to the slang words **beano** and **beaner** (as in 'party') entering the English language.

Individuals with a **zest** for life have energy and enthusiasm in spades. Keen to embark upon life's great adventure, they are also eager to infuse those around them with the same positive spirit. 'Bloody annoying' is another term for them, especially if you just wanted to be left in peace. Positive psychologists (yes, there is a body of people who call themselves that) regard 'zest' as one of the twenty-four key strengths or virtues possessed by humankind. It is a vital component, they insist, for experiencing a pleasurable, satisfying and meaningful existence. I, on the other hand, prefer my zest to be grated gently over a salad, added to any recipe involving fish, or squeezed into my vodka and soda, which is exactly what the French intended it for in the first place.

The word 'zest' – or *zeste*, 'peel', across the Channel – is of unknown origin but it was popularised by the French chefs of the great châteaux during the seventeenth century.

It was used in reference to orange or lemon peel, which had been found to lift and improve the taste of almost any sauce. The word began appearing in French cookery books in the 1690s and moved over to England a century later, where it took on an additional meaning of enthusiasm or keen enjoyment, alongside several other intensely annoying human attributes such as zeal, zip and zing.

Starbucks is, of course, the world's largest coffee-house chain, and the word is by now almost synonymous with 'coffee'. But it could all have been so different.

When teachers Zev Siegel and Jerry Baldwin first teamed up with writer Gordon Bowker to open their first coffee house in Seattle in 1971, one of the first decisions to be made was to agree on a catchy name for the new venture. A fan of Herman Melville's *Moby-Dick* (1851), Bowker originally suggested 'Pequod', the name of the whaling ship central to the story.

That was until someone pointed out that nobody would want to drink a steaming mug of 'pee-quod'. It was back to the drawing board. Staying with the theme of the novel, however, the team eventually settled on Starbuck, *Pequod*'s first mate, who was quite likely named after real-life nineteenth-century whaler Valentine Starbuck. I'm not sure they would have gone on to open 16,000 outlets worldwide if they'd stuck with their original suggestion.

When you are **hamstrung** you are prevented from doing something you had intended to do because of something outside your control. Hamstrings, as we know, are tendons at the back of the knee that connect the calf with the back of the thigh or 'ham'. The word is a reminder of days long gone when rural diets featured an awful lot of pork and legs of ham would be hung from a hook through the space between the thigh bone and tendons behind the knee.

In the days of medieval warfare, and hand-to-hand combat with swords and shields, it was a common battlefield tactic to approach an opponent from behind and slash him across the back of the thigh, severing the hamstrings and rendering him ineffective for the rest of the battle, or indeed the rest of his life. Pigs and other farmed animals could also be 'hamstrung' in this way when it was time for slaughter, rendering them incapable of wandering off or being stolen.

The word was notably used by John Milton in his 1641 pamphlet *Of Reformation in England*, in which he railed against church leaders who had 'hamstrung the valour of the subject by seeking to effeminate us all at home'. In modern times, any athlete can be metaphorically hamstrung (prevented from competing) by a literal hamstring injury. Just ask Michael Owen.

UNDER THE INFLUENCE

Everybody likes a little **tipple** every now and then. I know I do. The British are famously called a nation of drinkers, and there has historically been some truth to that, but we can take heart in the fact that the World Health Organization recently put Moldova in first place on the list of heavy-drinking countries: Moldovans drink, on average, 18.22 litres of (pure) alcohol per person per year. The UK trails way behind in lowly seventeenth position, following a handful of countries you wouldn't expect to find (Portugal, South Korea) and numerous countries you would (France, Ireland). That's pretty good going for a country that counts binge-drinking teens and the Scottish among its ranks.

Despite that setback, the wonderful English language has more words to describe overindulgence in my favourite pastime than any other in the world: 'bladdered', 'trolleyed', 'rat-arsed', 'tanked', 'plastered', 'hammered', 'steaming', 'leathered', 'juiced up' and 'pickled' are but a few that I dare to include, not to mention ADDLED, BEFUDDLED, BLOTTO, MULLERED, PIE-EYED and SOZZLED. But we have surprisingly few words to describe the very stuff that gets us into any of these conditions in the first place. The most popular, **booze**, evolved from the Middle English *bousen*, meaning 'to drink liquor', and is probably also related to the Old Dutch *busen*, meaning 'to drink to excess' (see BINGE). The other, slightly more genteel, word we use is 'tipple'.

In 1393, Richard II introduced new laws requiring all taverns to display a clear sign outside, to enable his official ale tasters to recognise the establishments and collect the appropriate taxes. This was the beginning of the British pub as we know it, but it was also the dawn of another quaint British tradition: the unlicensed drinking establishment (or private members' club, as the privileged like to call them). In around 1400, a 'tippling house' was an unlicensed place where alcohol could be bought in violation of the law. A 'tippler' was the owner of such a place and a 'tipple' was the tax-free HOOCH he sold. The expression probably came via the Vikings, possibly related to the Norwegian dialect word *tipla*, meaning 'to drink slowly'. These drinking dens became so popular during the Middle Ages that eventually even the tippler had to be licensed. Records reveal that, in 1577, five people in Boston, Lincolnshire, were granted tippling licences to sell Lincoln beer, and that any other tippler 'would only be able to do so under penalties'. But I doubt that stopped any of them.

We all have our **pipedreams** from time to time, fanciful ambitions that are usually too far beyond our reach to be achievable, but what do such dreams have to do with pipes? For the answer, we need to turn to the Victorian equivalent of modern-day 'crack', a drug that was also smoked in a pipe – opium.

It is commonly believed that London was the epicentre of the network of opium dens that spread throughout the world during the nineteenth century, when the Chinese trade in this drug – known for enhancing a person's thinking ability and heightening the imagination – was at its peak. But while it is true that London had its fair share of opium dens, the majority of those we have heard of are in fact fictional, the invention of influential writers of the age.

Sir Arthur Conan Doyle, Oscar Wilde and Charles Dickens all regularly used opium dens to set the scene for atmospheric tales of misadventure in the gloomy streets of the capital, but the city's Chinese community at the time never really consisted of more than a few hundred sailors who had either jumped ship or been left behind by mistake. This is in contrast to America, which became home to tens of thousands of Chinese immigrants during the nineteenth century, following the discovery of gold in 'them there hills' of California (see HOODLUM). But it was the romanticised version of London's illicit opium dens, in which men from every level of society, including the great and the good, could daydream for hours in an apparent state of euphoria, which led to 'pipedream' becoming an everyday expression. All of which makes me wonder what my granddad used to smoke in his pipe . . . He was usually away with the fairies.

In America anybody who has been drinking and is a little tipsy might be regarded as **sozzled**, while in Britain, by contrast, the word is usually applied only to the very drunk or inebriated. The *American Heritage Dictionary of the English Language*, first published in 1969, defines 'sozzle' as 'to splash, loll about and be lazy', all of which could describe a drunk. It's thought that this evolved from an older word, *soss*, which means 'to fall heavily and to splash in mud'. I can see a connection forming here . . .

Samuel Johnson, the great eighteenth-century British lexicographer and author of the first and most influential dictionary of the English language, defines the noun 'soss' as 'a lazy fellow, a lush'. The verb 'to soss', he says, probably evolved from the French word *sous* or 'under' and meant 'to fall' in the sense of 'to fall heavily into a chair'. It is therefore easy to see how the word 'sozzled', meaning 'drunk' and therefore inclined to fall over − whether or not a chair is conveniently stationed next to you − could have evolved from there.

A **tumbler** can be an acrobat; a pigeon that can perform a sort of victory roll in flight; part of a lock; some sort of car or tank (for Batman fans); or (for me) a flat-bottomed whisky glass made from plastic, metal or glass. The latter is the tumbler we are interested in here, because rarely has an object been so inappropriately named. Or, at least, that's what I thought.

The earliest examples of what we would call a tumbler would have been found in any Roman household during the pre-Christian period. Thanks to the glass-blowing methods at the time, many of them had a slightly rounded bottom if they hadn't been flattened out properly when the glass was still hot. Some crafty innkeepers would only buy these 'faulty' glasses, ensuring that customers had to keep hold of their mugs at all times to prevent them from 'tumbling over', which naturally led to more drinking. But the first reference to a small glass being called a tumbler is during the seventeenth century when ones made from Venetian glass were advertised, glassmaking being one of Venice's oldest trades.

Mass production of the tumbler began in the 1820s when Deming Jarves, founder of the Boston and Sandwich Glass Company in Massachusetts, produced the first pressed-glass water tumbler by forcing molten glass into a specially constructed iron mould. This technique not only ensured the standardisation of tumbler quality and size for the first time, but also ensured that they had perfectly flat bottoms and would never tumble over again. Perhaps we should all raise a glass to Deming Jarves for saving us all from financial ruin down the local.

Blotto is thought to have been used in England since shortly before the First World War to describe a drunk, somebody who has been on the sauce for a while. But I am unable to find any evidence confirming its use before 1917, when it appeared in a story by an Englishman living in Paris, who sadly didn't reveal how he'd first come across this strange but oddly appropriate word.

While many people assume that 'blotto' must derive from 'blot', as in the verb meaning 'to absorb liquid', a more compelling explanation lies in the French company Blotto Frères, one of the largest manufacturers of delivery tricycles during the early twentieth century. Blotto's three-wheelers competed in the popular Triporteur races, held annually from 1901 over a course between Paris and Versailles and which became so popular that they led to the inaugural Tour de France in 1903. During the First World War, Blotto Frères tricycles became a regular feature on the frontline, with thousands of them delivering daily supplies to the troops. But their unusual backwards design – two wheels at the front to support the delivery basket and one at the rear – made them notoriously unstable and difficult to control, and they must have presented a hilarious spectacle for onlookers as they wobbled around and tipped over in the mud.

This would explain how the word 'blotto' became associated with a reeling drunk, but it was a Laurel and Hardy movie released in 1930 and simply called *Blotto* that lifted the word from relative obscurity. The film features Stan and Ollie getting riotously drunk at a Prohibition-era speakeasy before realising they are only drinking cold tea, the WHISKEY having been replaced by Stan's wife. The film is a timeless comedy classic that brought a valuable word to the English language – and all thanks to a French tricycle maker.

Just as a nod to the scientific community, 'blotto' is also an acronym for 'Bovine Lacto Transfer Technique Optimiser',

a blocking reagent, whatever that is. But I'm sure you all knew that already.

The word **piggyback** is not connected to small-scale medieval banking systems (see PIGGYBANK) and neither has it anything to do with riding a certain kind of farmyard animal. It actually derives from the phrase 'pick a back', in reference to a person choosing who should carry them home from the alehouse after they have become **pie-eyed** on the local brew. 'Pie-eyed' is itself a popular expression, one that has been in use since the early part of the twentieth century. Most people, when in the sort of condition that might require them to 'pick a back', find it hard to focus their eyes, which isn't really surprising since they're watery and bloodshot and presumably resemble the innards of some sort of pie. (Although I can't think which one, and I certainly wouldn't want to eat it.)

The first known record of 'pie-eyed' in print came in 1904, when American humorist George Ade used it in his book *Breaking into Society*: 'They sat down with him at the table and inhaled the Scotch until they were all pie-eyed.' The expression subsequently made it to Hollywood: in 1959, legendary composer and band leader Duke Ellington played a roadhouse owner called Pie-Eye in the BLOCKBUSTER *The Anatomy of a Murder*, starring James Stewart.

When somebody is **befuddled** they are either confused and unable to think clearly or they've been drinking (which, I am told, can lead to a similar state of mind). *A New English Dictionary on Historical Principles*, the precursor to the *Oxford English Dictionary*, defined the word in the late nineteenth century in such a way as to suggest the 'be' of 'befuddled' was a prefix and 'fuddled' a word in its own right. The dictionary did not expand on this, sadly, but there is evidence to suggest that, as far back as 1588 (the year of the Spanish Armada, in case you were wondering why that date is familiar), the words 'fuddle' and 'fuddled' denoted alcohol and drunkenness. An early edition of the *Oxford English Dictionary* defines 'befuddled' as: 'To make stupid with tippling, also to stupefy. Hence befuddlement; intoxication, confusion or stupefaction.'

Grogblossoms are, or used to be, blotches, boils or other general patches of redness on the face and nose due to alcoholic overindulgence. The related word **groggy** means to feel run-down and unwell, also as the result of drinking far too much, while **grog**, unsurprisingly, is the beverage responsible for all these ailments. But who or what was the original grog?

The word entered the English language thanks to an admiral named Edward Vernon (1684–1757), who styled his entire naval career on that of his personal hero, Sir Francis Drake, which is to say he harassed the Spanish at every opportunity. He fought in Gibraltar, Barcelona and Malaga in 1704–5, and later seized Portobello, a silver-exporting port on the Spanish-held coast of Panama. His fleet completely destroyed the port, decimating the Spanish economy in the process, which was deemed such a spectacular triumph that he became a national hero. Portobello Road, home to one of London's best-known markets, is named after this.

During the raid on Portobello, incidentally, Vernon commanded a young soldier from the American colonies called Lawrence Washington, whose brother George later became the first president of the United States. The elder Washington named the family home Mount Vernon after his commanding officer, and it was there that President Washington, sworn enemy of the British, spent his later years. It is not known whether he appreciated the irony.

But perhaps Vernon's greatest achievement came during his time in the West Indies, when he replaced the neat rum that was issued to sailors twice daily with a watered-down version laced with lime, to prevent scurvy. (Which, by the way, is the reason why the Americans call the British LIMEYS.) The admiral had by this time earned the affectionate NICKNAME 'Old Grog' thanks to his trademark grogram coat (from the French *gros grain*, 'course grain': a rough mixture of mohair and silk), and the name was soon transferred to the concoction he had created. The origin of the term was later immortalised by a sailor called Thomas Trotter in a poem he wrote in 1781:

A mighty bowl on deck he drew
And filled it to the brink,
Such drank the *Burford*'s gallant crew
And such the gods shall drink.

The sacred robe which Vernon wore
Was drenched within the same,
And hence his virtues guard our shore
And Grog derives its name.

The word **mullered** – particularly prevalent in Scotland and the north of England – has two usages, although they are related. The first is to indicate something that has been totally destroyed, perhaps a car or a sports team, and the second is to describe a person who is very drunk. Used in this way, it first came to prominence in the early 1990s, but the *Chambers Dictionary of Slang* reveals it was a well-known prison term during the 1950s, denoting an inmate who had been badly beaten. It is generally believed that the word evolved from the Middle English regional verb *mullen*, meaning 'to grind or crumble'. This sounds much more likely than the supposed link with the ROMANY word *mul*, 'to die', and definitely more plausible than the link, favoured in some quarters, with Islam and *mullahed*, which isn't even a real word.

Hooch is a crude but powerful homemade alcoholic drink whose heyday was during Prohibition in the United States

(1920–33). The word was inspired by the Hutsnuwu tribe of Native Americans (the name means 'grizzly bear fort'), who in the nineteenth century had a reputation for drunken rowdiness, as a result of which they were being closely monitored in the Alaskan reservations they had been confined to by European settlers.

In his study of the region, *Alaska and Missions on the North Pacific Coast* (1880), Presbyterian missionary Sheldon Jackson (1834–1909) anglicised the name of the tribe, introducing a new word to the English language in the process. According to his account: 'On Tuesday we reached Angoon, the chief town of the Hootznahoos [which sounds like something Billy Connolly might say on a drunken night out – this is my observation, not Jackson's], but we did not remain for long as the whole town was drunk.' Jackson went on to blame the liquor for 'nearly all of the trouble in the country', concluding that 'the cause of the disturbance was, as usual, Hoochinoo'. Which was not entirely fair as, although the Native Americans were by then distilling their own alcohol, it was the European settlers who must have taught them the technique in the first place. However, the name stuck and within ten years the expression 'hooch' was commonly being used to describe illegal liquor, which became in high demand when Prohibition struck. (See also BOOTLEGGERS.)

Sir Oswald **Binge** (1678–1768) was a country squire from Leicestershire who was well known for his epic eating and drinking sessions. He could famously remain at the dining table for days at a time while his guests came and went; despite his doctor's warnings to the contrary, he lived until a ripe old age. Sadly, the only reference I can find to Sir Oswald is in relation to this story, and that, by definition, makes it extremely unlikely as a source for the term associated with his surname.

Until around the mid-nineteenth century, to 'binge' was to fill the bottom of a boat with water to allow the timbers to expand when repairs were needed, or simply to flush out the hull. Bingeing, or soaking, a vessel was common seafaring practice in the days of wooden-framed ships, and

sailors who lived long before Sir Oswald munched his way through Leicestershire were known to have been **on a binge** if they had cleaned out a wooden barrel of rum. So let's leave Sir Oswald Binge and his fictitious friends to the interwebbers to discuss and move on to another entry.

If a person's brain is **addled**, he or she is confused or unable to think coherently. 'Addled' is often used to mean 'drunk', and the symptoms are certainly similar. The ineffective second parliament of King James I, which sat between 5 April and 7 June 1614 and was dissolved by the king after it failed to agree to a grant of substantial funds, was famously NICKNAMED the Addled Parliament.

The word 'addle' itself is related to the Old English *adela*, 'farmyard dung'. Rotten eggs were being referred to as 'addled' as early as the thirteenth century, thanks to their terrible manure-like smell. Any modern-day drunk who is too confused to do anything effectively can therefore thank James I's useless Addled ('Rotten') Parliament for lending its name to describe the 'manure-like' state of his mind.

When something is described as having **legs** it will last for a long time, such as a story in the news that is sufficiently scandalous or horrifying that it may 'run and run'. To have 'great legs' is something else entirely, and I don't just mean one of the attributes of a CORKER – although corks do come into it. I'm referring here to the wine industry, which is well known for the absurd-looking methods wine tasters adopt when deciding if a bottle is worth quaffing. But there is in fact a very good reason for the 'sniff, swirl, spit or swallow' method of wine tasting that makes such entertaining TV. A taster first needs to look at the clarity of the wine and then smell it to check there are no problems due to refermentation or bacterial contamination. The wine then needs to be swirled around the glass, which will leave trickles of wine appearing to run down the sides of the glass. These are known in the trade as 'legs' (or 'tears'). Thick and easily identifiable legs indicate a high level of alcohol. To declare that a wine has got 'great legs', therefore, is to opine that it is rich, dense and full of body, although, with the high alcohol content, you'd be advised not to drink too much or you could end up **legless**.

LOVE AND LUST

Canoodling is a fabulous word that describes a kiss and a cuddle between two people – if it goes any further than that, an entirely different range of words becomes more appropriate.

There is a wonderful story behind this word, harking back to the days when a young lady of a certain class would require a chaperone when taking an afternoon walk by the river with a potential suitor, the perfect gentleman, before retiring for tea with her sisters and aunts while the bloke went off to meet his mates down the club and roar it up with dancing girls until the wee small hours. After a few months, the chaperone would begin to keep a discreet distance (see GOOSEBERRY) while the courting couple hopped into a boat – a canoe, as it happens – and paddled off to a quiet spot to get to know one another a little better, that is, to 'canoodle'.

I would love that to be true but I think we can all agree that it can't be. For a start, it may not even be British in origin. When the journalist George Augustus Sala used the word 'canoodling' in an article he contributed to Charles Dickens's journal *Household Words* in 1859, he credited it to 'our American cousins'. And he is probably right – but it seems our American cousins had themselves borrowed it from elsewhere, namely Germany, following the great German migration to the States during the nineteenth century (see also DUDE). The origin of 'canoodle' would appear to be *knudeln*, a slang German word for 'to cuddle'.

I have discovered some correspondence in support of this theory between none other than the eminent etymologist W. E. Umbach and Thomas Middleton, writer of a column about language in the *Saturday Review of Literature* during the 1970s. 'I referred to the old *Muret-Sanders Encyclopaedic Dictionary*,' writes Umbach, 'and found, to my delight, "knudeln", which is defined as "to cuddle". It is almost impossible to escape the conclusion that it was one of the German words brought by German immigrants who came to the Missouri and Mississippi Basin in the years following the Revolution of 1848.'

Canoes, indeed!

The blushing **bride** may well have something to be embarrassed about when she finds out that the word derives from the distinctly alcoholic-sounding *bride-ale*, Old English for 'wedding feast'. There were many 'ales' during the merry old Middle Ages, all of them related to some occasion for a boozy knees-up in the parish. The *leet-ale* was drunk up at the local manor house, the *church-ale* and *clerk-ale* were, well, let's just say religious celebrations, while a *bid-ale* was a celebration in honour of an individual.

The **bridegroom** is the lucky chap who gets to spend months on end choosing seasonal flowers and meaningful hymns, all of which go spectacularly unnoticed by the male half of the congregation come the big day. All in all, a bridegroom has a thankless task – but an interesting name. The Old English word for a man marrying his sweetheart is *brydguma*, which literally means 'bride man'. However, over the years the *guma* part of the word, which means 'man', has become confused with the word 'groom', which originally meant 'manservant'. 'I now pronounce you bride and manservant.' (Insert obvious joke here.)

Which brings us of course to the word **husband**, which some people believe must be related to 'housebound', in the sense that the married man is saddled with the responsibility of providing a home for his family. The word is in fact Norse in origin, its roots going back to the Viking occupation of England between the eighth and eleventh centuries. Their word *husbondi*, from *hus* (house) and *bondi* (the man who dwells in it), which firmly places the married man at the head of the household, evolved into the Old English *husbonda*. The Old English word *wif*, by contrast, is thought to have been adapted from Old High German, in which *wib* meant 'veiled one'. Tracing the word **wife** further back, however, it basically just means 'woman', still reflected in words like **fishwife** and **midwife** (literally 'with woman' in Middle English).

These days a **honeymoon** is the holiday that newly married couples take directly after their wedding. The first suggestion for its origin takes us to Egypt, nowadays a popular honeymoon destination, where in ancient times it was customary for the BRIDE's father to give his new son-in-law a month's supply of mead, a type of wine made from honey. That period became known as the 'honeymoon' (literally 'honey month').

There is a second explanation, however, that stems from a more recent period of European history. Going back a few hundred years, it was once customary for newly married couples to share a drink of diluted honey during the first month of wedlock, to symbolise the 'sweetness' of those early few weeks. As a result, the word 'honeymoon' was in regular use by the mid-sixteenth century; two centuries later, it was defined by Dr Johnson in his *Dictionary of the English Language* as 'the first month after marriage when there is nothing but tenderness and pleasure'. Either way, it's interesting to see how realistic we have historically been about the longevity of marital bliss.

Floozie is another word for much the same type of girl as a BIMBO or SLAPPER. The expression is thought to have evolved from the old English word *floosy*, meaning 'fluffy', before acquiring its less innocuous meaning as a slang term for 'prostitute'. The word caused a stir in America in 1938, when it appeared in the title of a song by JAZZ legend Slim Gaillard: 'Flat Foot Floozie (with a Floy Floy)'. Gaillard had to change 'floozie' to 'floogie' to enable the song to get radio play, especially since 'floy floy' was slang for a sexually transmitted disease. Imagine today releasing a song called 'Flat Foot Bimbo with the Clap'.

These days the expression **bimbo** is applied to an above-average-looking woman with below-average intelligence, often with even lower standards of behaviour. The word was first used as an insult in 1929, in the popular American musical *The Broadway Melody*, the first 'talkie' to win Best Picture at the Academy Awards. In one scene the central character angrily calls a chorus girl a 'bimbo', and such was the popularity of the film that the word has been used in a derogatory fashion ever since. The film was clearly the word's turning point, since the *Oxford English Dictionary* of the same year defined 'bimbo' as simply a 'woman'.

What is less clear is how the word, to mean a certain sort of woman, disappeared for several decades during the middle of the twentieth century. In 1956, country and western star Jim Reeves had a hit with 'Bimbo', a sing-along

57

cowboy song about a little boy with millions of friends. Around the same time there was quite a proliferation of stars of above-average beauty, below-average intelligence and almost no morals – Marilyn Monroe springs to mind – and they were not called 'bimbos' but 'dumb blondes'. The bimbo was back by the 1980s, however, and the more recent rise of reality TV has very much reclaimed the word for the girl with below-average everything – I'm not convinced even good looks matter much these days.

What is hard to understand is how 'bimbo' became associated with women in the first place: only a decade before its first outing on Broadway, it was a commonly used Italian-American slang word for an uneducated man who lacked manners and was generally rough and loutish. The word is a contraction of the Italian *bambino*, 'male child', the female equivalent being *bambina*. So basically when we call a woman a bimbo, we are technically calling her a little boy – something she presumably doesn't resemble in the slightest.

The word **adultery** is sternly defined in the 1828 edition of *Webster's American Dictionary of the English Language* as 'violation of the marriage bed'. Although indulged in only by adults, that has nothing to do with the etymology of the term. Instead, for the root of the word, we must travel back through Old French to the Latin *adulterare*, which translates as 'to corrupt or to debase', and not just in the sense of one person corrupting or debasing another, but also with the idea of the 'purity' of the offspring in a marriage being affected – 'adulterated' – when you no longer know who the father is.

From here, it's a short hop to **divorce**, which evolved from another Latin word, *divortium*, meaning a fork in the road – a literal parting of the ways – and providing the root of the modern English word 'diversion'.

The Americans best explain what happens in the marriage cycle after DIVORCE, with their word **alimony**, defined as an 'allowance for support, especially for a wife by a husband after a divorce'. This word looks as though it should be connected to 'money' in some fashion, but instead it can be traced to the Latin *alimonia*, 'sustenance', which in turn is connected with the verb *alere*, 'to feed', hence 'alimentation' or sustenance of a more literal kind.

The best advice to give here, of course, is: 'try **monogamy**', meaning 'only one partner at a time' or 'don't cheat on your wife, you idiot'. Monogamy is as old as the human race, while the word itself is made up of two ancient Greek ones: *mono*, 'alone', and *gamas*, 'marriage'.

The word **tomboy**, denoting a young girl who behaves more like a boy, can be traced back to the sixteenth century. It comes from the Anglo-Saxon *tumbere*, 'dancer' or 'romper', which is from the same root as the French *tomber*, 'to fall', and also related to *tom rig*, a seventeenth-century term for a prostitute or 'loose woman'. The 'rig' part is from the French *rigoler*, 'to make merry'. Meanwhile, Down Under, the phrase 'tom tart' was regularly used to describe a lady, loose or otherwise, possibly as a result of COCKNEY rhyming slang (tom tart = sweetheart), while in America the expression 'tommy' meant 'romping girl'. Back in London, Cockney rhyming slang came up with 'tommy tucker' as a term for a loose woman, so it's easy to see how the current slang term **tom**, for 'prostitute', came about.

A **corker** is an outstanding or excellent film, golf shot, person, etc. Obviously none of these things have anything to do with corks, but a leading theory as to the word's etymology does take us back to Cork in Ireland.

According to the story, the remnants of the defeated Spanish Armada escaped into the North Sea in 1588, went around Scotland and headed south through the Irish Sea in the direction of Spain, with their sails between their legs. In September of that year, a combination of navigational errors and severe North Atlantic storms swept most of the bedraggled Spanish ships on to the rocks around the city of Cork, and it was here that many took refuge and hid from the English among the Irish community. The inevitable interbreeding between the Spanish and Irish created a new generation of exotic-looking half-Mediterranean offspring in the County Cork area, the female half of which became known as 'corkers', meaning 'beautiful women'.

It's a good story, but it isn't true, I'm afraid. In the first place, the Spanish fleet did not enter the Irish Sea, but instead took a course around the west coast of Ireland, where they were driven on to the rocks by storms. This would have made their subsequent offspring 'tralees', 'kilkees' or 'dingles'! Secondly, while some were hidden by the Irish before becoming part of the Irish army, the vast majority either drowned or were caught and killed by the English. There was no generation of exotic-looking Cork girls, as any visitor to Cork will confirm.

Instead, the original definition of 'corker' was in the context of a 'hard or finishing blow' (see also HAYMAKER). It was used as a boxing term as recently as 1936, as P. G. Wodehouse, author of the Jeeves and Wooster novels, demonstrated in *Laughing Gas*: 'Nine times out of ten [fights] are absolute washouts. But this one was a real corker.' Boxing fans around this time would regard the big knockout punch as the one that 'put the cork in it'.

There is, however, earlier evidence of 'corker' being used to describe an attractive woman, the connection between the two definitions presumably being that a beautiful woman is 'a real knockout'. An American music-hall song of 1891, entitled 'My Gal's a Corker', opens with the lines: 'My gal's a corker, she's a New Yorker, / I buy her everything to keep her in style.'

A **bachelor** is a man who is lucky enough to have remained unmarried. The word comes from the Old French *bacheler*, which somehow evolved from the Latin *baccalaris*, meaning 'farm worker'. The word was first used in English during the great age of chivalry in the late Middle Ages, when a Knight Bachelor was a young man who aspired to become a knight but was too young to display his own heraldic emblem. A sort of student knight, if you will. In those days, 'bachelors' were very keen to lose their bachelor status, although their modern-day counterparts seem to be in no hurry at all.

To play the **gooseberry** is to be an awkward third party in the company of two lovers. It's not an ideal situation to find yourself in, but we've all been there at one time or another. One suggestion for why we use the word in this context is that Old Gooseberry was once a euphemism for the devil, and obviously nobody wanted to be in the company of that particular mythical beast. While that last part is true, there is no solid evidence to support this theory. There was a card game called 'old gooseberry' in the late eighteenth century, in which it is possible that the gooseberry in question was the Joker – that is, the odd one out – but this too is conjecture. Another theory, included by Eric Partridge in the 1837 edition of his *Dictionary of Unconventional English*, suggests the popular DESSERT **gooseberry fool** as the origin, and that the unwanted third part was just that: a fool.

A more compelling explanation is that, in the gentle days of the eighteenth century, a young lady would often require the services of a chaperone if she wanted to step out with a gentleman for a walk on a warm summer's afternoon. Often the accompanying escort would be a trusted old aunt or housekeeper, who would keep at a discreet distance from the couple, perhaps by wandering off on the pretext of

picking wild gooseberries. Certainly by the mid-nineteenth century, chaperones and escorts were informally known as 'gooseberry pickers', which seems to back this story up. The 1898 edition of *Brewer's Dictionary of Phrase and Fable* defines 'gooseberry picker' as 'anyone who has the toil of picking a troublesome fruit for the delectation of others', but personally I prefer the story about the old aunt off picking gooseberries while her young charge got up to no good.

STUFF AND NONSENSE

Gibberish, to describe meaningless statements or nonsense remarks, made its first appearance in the English language in the early sixteenth century. It is popularly thought to have some connection with the eighth-century Persian alchemist Jabir ibn Hayyan, later Latinised as 'Geber', whose complex and impenetrable works supposedly gave rise to the expression 'Geber-like' or 'Geber-ish' among those attempting to study them.

Another theory, also related to the Middle East, is that the word can be traced to the Arabic place name Jabal-Tariq, 'Mountain of Tariq', now more commonly known as Gibraltar. Natives of 'the Rock', while officially British, tend to be bilingual, peppering their speech with Spanish words and phrases and even starting a sentence in one language and finishing it in another, which outsiders have always found hard to understand, dismissing their vocabulary as 'Gibraltar-ish' and subsequently 'Gibberish'.

While Jabir ibn Hayyan did indeed exist – and had his work copied in the thirteenth century by a writer calling himself 'Geber' – it seems odd that the word 'gibberish', if it can be attributed to him, took so many centuries to enter the English language. He is therefore unlikely to be the source of the word. And as for the Gibraltar theory: it's far-fetched, to say the least. Much more plausible is the suggestion that the expression evolved from the late fifteenth-century word 'jabber', still used today and meaning 'to talk nonsense', which was of course popularised a few centuries later by Lewis Carroll in his bestselling book *Through the Looking Glass* (1871), via the title of one of his most famous nonsense poems, 'Jabberwocky'.

A definition of **babbling** is a young child's early attempts at language – one level up from pointing and shouting but still one below the use of recognisable words. That said, we do also describe any adult talking inarticulately as babbling. But where does the word actually come from?

There is the story in the Book of Genesis describing how descendants of survivors of the Great Flood built a city and huge tower with which they thought they could reach heaven. God was so angered by their presumption, according to the story, that in retaliation he caused the builders, who previously all spoke one language, to speak in different tongues, so that they could not communicate with one another and hence complete their vainglorious project. The city was thenceforth called Babel, from the Hebrew *babal*, meaning 'to jumble', and the word **babel** entered the English language in the sixteenth century to indicate 'a confusion of sounds'. By the seventeenth century, it was being used to describe any noisy assembly of people where no individual words could be identified.

Although 'babble' sounds as though it ought to come from 'babel', there is little evidence that it actually does, however. It's more likely that the word evolved from Middle Low German for 'to prattle', *babbelen*, based in turn upon the repeated 'ba-ba-ba' sounds made by a baby or young child. Like the builders of the biblical tower, all babies speak the same language, it would seem, as 'babble' is very similar in French (*babiller*), Icelandic (*babbla*) and even Sanskrit (*balbala*). Another word for a general uproar, **hubbub**, sounds as though it too should be related to 'babel', but it most likely comes from *ubub*, a Scottish Gaelic cry of aversion or contempt, probably against the English.

Gobbledygook, meaningless or jargon-filled language, was claimed by an American politician, Maury Maverick, to have been made up by him when he banned all 'gobbledygook language' in a memo he sent in March 1944 to employees in the Smaller War Plants Corporation, of which he was chairman. As Maury, himself the grandson of Samuel, the original MAVERICK, explained to a *New York Times* reporter in May that same year: 'People ask me where I got gobbledygook from and I do not know. It must have come in a vision. Perhaps I was thinking of the old bearded turkey gobbler back in Texas, who was always gobbledy-gobbling and strutting with curious pomposity. At the end of this gobble there was always some sort of gook.'

Right then, so let's clear this up for the good old Texan visionary. There is an alternative theory that the word instead evolved during the French Indochina War, when French soldiers encountered the Thai and Vietnamese people for the first time and supposedly referred to their language as *gobble de gouke*, or 'gooks' gobble'. This theory is dubious enough even before we remind ourselves, as American etymologists like to, that the French Indochina War began in 1946, two years after Maverick's famed memo, which seems to indicate that this fabulous word is of American origin.

The word 'gook' on its own, however, appears to have been in circulation among French troops before Maury Maverick was born, let alone busy writing memos. The French took control of Northern Vietnam after victory over China in the Sino-French War of 1884–5, and popularly NICKNAMED any Asian prostitute, soldier or other undesirable a 'gook'. As a first lieutenant during the First World War, Maverick is likely to have added the word to his vocabulary when serving alongside French soldiers. Visions indeed?

Balderdash is a fine old English word used to describe utter nonsense. It is thought by some etymologists to have evolved from the Old Welsh term *baldorduss*, meaning 'idle chatter', a word that in turn probably led to the English equivalent, BABBLING.

It's more likely, however, that 'balderdash' emerged during the sixteenth century to describe an unpleasant mixture of frothy liquids. Used in this way, the word appears in Tobias Smollett's *Travels through France and Italy* of 1776, in which the author condemns some of the wine he encounters along the way: 'The winemakers of Nice brew a balderdash and even mix it with pigeon dung and quick-lime.'

So in 1776 balderdash meant some kind of drink, and unpalatable at that. By 1917, when the 'Sage of Baltimore', H. L. Mencken, published his groundbreaking book *In Defense of Women*, the meaning of the word had clearly moved on, although it was still negative. Mencken used it in his book to criticise businessmen, stating: 'Their very ability to master and retain such balderdash as constitutes their stock in trade is proof of their inferior mentality [to women].'

The true origin of the word, according to one theory, can be traced as far back as the twelfth century and the Norse god of light, Balder – slain, in Norse legend, by a rival in love, his brother the blind god Hod. Meanwhile, 'dash' derives from the Middle English *dashen*, meaning 'to strike forcibly' against something, as in 'dashing one's hopes'

– as Balder's clearly would have been. Sounds like balderdash to me.

In America, **Poppycock** is a well-known brand of popcorn that was created by Harold Vair during the 1950s. In 1960, a Swiss company bought the distribution rights to Poppycock and it remains a popular brand to this day. But I wonder if Harold Vair would have given his popcorn this name if he had been aware of the usage of the word in Britain, to describe something as utterly nonsensical, or if he had known the exact derivation of the term. The word came into existence in the eighteenth century, after British sailors adopted a regional Dutch word, *pappekak*, meaning 'soft' (*pap*) 'dung' (*kak*), which they used as a mild expletive or to point out that someone was talking a load of you-know-what. In South Africa, the word *kak* is still used by Afrikaners, themselves descended from the Dutch, in much the same way.

It is assumed in some parts of America that the word **tomfoolery** – to mean high-spirited or silly behaviour (see also SHENANIGANS) – originated in the Southern states, in connection with slavery and the derogatory NICKNAME 'Uncle Tom'. A second American connection offers another theory for the origin of the term, namely a popular racehorse called Tom Fool from the 1950s, who won many major races during his career and came in at number eleven on the list of thoroughbred American champions of the twentieth century.

But 'tomfoolery' was in fact recorded in England long before the height of the slave trade, and certainly long before that particular racehorse was speeding around the track. Its origin lies in William Shakespeare's tragedy of 1606, *King Lear*, in which Tom the Fool plays a central role. In so naming the character, the Bard was paying tribute to one of his close friends, Tom Skelton, a court jester – believed to be the last in English history – at Muncaster Castle near Ravenglass in Cumbria who was popularly known as Tom the Fool.

In real life, it appears that Tom was a much more sinister character than perhaps even his playwright friend realised and not averse to a spot of very dirty work on behalf of his employer, Sir Ferdinand Pennington. It is said that on one occasion he murdered an apprentice carpenter on the orders of Sir Ferdinand after the lad was caught in a clinch with Pennington's daughter. Skelton decapitated him as he slept in a stable block and the famous head-carrying ghost is said still to haunt the grounds to this day.

Skelton was also known to spend many hours under a tree on the road to Ravenglass, greeting travellers as they passed. Those Tom warmed to were directed to the ford over the River Esk while those he disliked were pointed in the direction of a hidden quicksand and bog marsh. Not all lived to tell the tale. Tom Skelton himself died in 1600, a victim, legend has it, of the very same quicksand, after losing his way back to the castle after a night in a local tavern. A portrait of Tom 'the Fool' Skelton still hangs in Muncaster Castle along with the original copy of his will. The present owners – descendants of the vindictive Pennington – claim that the spirit of Tom the Fool still lives at the castle and is responsible for much of the ghostly tomfoolery supposedly going on there to this day.

To be **agog** is to be in a state of bewilderment or anticipation, perhaps staring wide-eyed (GOOGLY-EYED, even) at something happening in front of you. The root of this funny-looking word is the Old French expression *en gogues*, which meant 'in merriment'.

It has been suggested that the behaviour of the inhabitants of Ballyhooly in County Cork, Ireland, provides the derivation for the word **ballyhoo**, to describe rowdy antics or a noisy uproar, but allow me to free the quiet villagers from this stigma once and for all. The term appears in fact to have evolved from the native Central American word *ballahou*, a type of wood used to build clumsy and hard-to-handle sailing boats. This word gave rise to the sailing expression **ballyhoo of blazes**, used contemptuously by seafarers to describe an inferior type of boat. Meanwhile, a *ballahoo* is still a type of fast schooner used in the West Indies and Bermuda.

A **flibbertigibbet** is a quirky sort of person, generally a bit flighty and unreliable. The word was immortalised in song in the 1965 film classic *The Sound of Music*, in which two nuns try to sum up the character of the high-spirited young woman seeking to join their order. 'How do you find a word that means "Maria"?' sings one, to which 'Flibbertigibbet' is the reply.

The word is particularly common in Yorkshire but it has

southern associations too. As noted by the distinguished historian John Yonge in 1847, Flibbertigibbet was the name of the impish apprentice of the blacksmith Wayland from Norse mythology. According to legend, Wayland's Smithy, a megalithic long barrow or tomb situated close to the famous Uffington White Horse hill carving on the Berkshire Downs, is where he had his forge.

Sir Walter Scott used Flibbertigibbet as a NICKNAME for Dickie Sludge, the shambling urchin in his 1821 novel *Kenilworth*, and over two centuries before that, Shakespeare employed it as the name for one of the five fiends who supposedly torment Edgar in *King Lear* (1605), borrowing the word from *A Declaration of Egregious Popish Impostures*, a religious tract written by Samuel Harsnett two years earlier.

But where did the word itself come from? One theory is that it evolved from an older expression, 'fly in the gibbet' – a reference to the body of an executed outlaw displayed in the gibbet (gallows) outside the town in which he had committed his crime. This was a common practice during the sixteenth and seventeenth centuries, designed to serve as a deterrent for others in the days before transportation to Australia had been invented. A second theory is that the expression was originally nautical, related to the jib of a sailing ship that has become loose and is flapping in the wind, although I feel it is far more likely to have something to do with the poor soul left dangling from the gibbet.

Kerfuffle is the sort of expression my nan would use to describe the Blitz (see BLIZZARD). A relatively new word, first recorded around the end of the Second World War, it describes some sort of commotion or confrontation. It comes from Scots Gaelic, one of the many languages that have mixed and merged over the centuries to form what we now call English. The Scottish *curfuffle* is itself a combination of *car*, 'twisted' in Gaelic, and *fuffle*, which translates as 'dishevelled'.

Claptrap is another of those wonderful words used to dismiss someone's opinion as utter nonsense. Indeed, when it comes to the words we use to describe something we don't believe, 'claptrap' is in excellent company: BALDERDASH and POPPYCOCK are notable examples, along with BALONEY, BOLLOCKS, CODSWALLOP and FIDDLESTICKS.

But what did 'claptrap' mean originally? Well, it appears that one type of claptrap – or rather 'clap-trap' – was a mechanical device, invented by a Drury Lane stagehand in the mid-nineteenth century, which simulated the sound of hand-clapping, presumably to encourage it among members of the audience. It was not unlike the modern-day canned laughter that winds us all up on bad TV sitcoms. The falseness of the applause may well have been the inspiration for the word we still use today.

This story may well be true but the word itself is actually much older than that. Nathan Bailey's *A Universal Etymological*

English Dictionary, which was published in London in 1731 and went on to become the most popular dictionary of the day – quite some achievement considering how that century also produced Samuel Johnson – defines 'claptrap' as: 'A name given to the rant and rhymes that dramatic writers, to please the actors, allow them to go off [stage] with, as much as to say it is a trap to catch a clap, by way of applause from the spectators at a play.' This definition of the word was clearly still very much in use – and across the pond, no less – a century later, as recorded in an article from an 1835 edition of the *New England* magazine in which the writer complains that, in order to appease the lead actor in a play, a 'piece must abound in claptraps'.

In time, these 'claptraps' – rousing speeches or topical jokes designed to elicit applause – became as unpopular among 'serious' actors and critics as the aforementioned mechanical device for manufacturing applause, although you'll still hear plenty of them at the Christmas pantomime.

'I've told you **umpteen** times' is a despairing statement many of us are familiar with. 'Umpteen' signifies an unspecified large number that can never be verified (see also NTH, X, X-RAY). It is a variation on *umpty*, meaning much the same thing, which found its way into the English language towards the end of the nineteenth century. It is generally believed that *umpty* became a slang term for a single dash in Morse Code during the First World War, before being superseded by 'umpteen', which borrowed its suffix from the 'teens' and alluded to a large, unspecified number of dashes in a sequence. Which may well account for some of the communications cock-ups during that particular military catastrophe.

Rigmarole, denoting a tediously complex procedure, is an unusual-sounding word from the mid-eighteenth century, while the origin of the term goes back well over 700 years. It dates to 1296, when the Scottish noblemen signed deeds of loyalty to King Edward I of England. They all fixed their seals to the deeds, which collectively became known as the Ragman Roll or Ragman's Roll, either in reference to the ribbons (or 'rags') attached to some of the seals or to an earlier census collector called Rageman or Ragemund. Around the same time, *ragman* was a slang word for the devil (see RAGAMUFFIN), which may well have been the Scots' NICKNAME for the hated English king.

Either way, there is little doubt that the process of getting the Scots to sign deeds of loyalty to England, and subsequently having to assemble the deeds into one forty-foot-long document for the king, was quite some rigmarole.

Hunky-dory is a word we use to describe a satisfactory position. All is well with the world. It is also the title of David Bowie's fourth studio album, released in December 1971, but you won't be surprised to hear that Bowie did not invent the word. It does, however, have a much earlier association with music. In 1862, American songwriter George Christy published a collection of songs under the title *George Christy's Essence of Old Kentucky*, which included a song called 'Hunkey-Dory':

> One of the boys am I
> That always am in clover;
> With spirits light and high,
> It's well I'm known all over.
> I am always to be found
> A singing in my glory;
> With your smiling faces round,
> It's when I'm hunkey-dory.

The song was performed by the Christy Minstrels, a 'blackface' minstrel group created by Christy's father, Edwin P. Christy. The Christy Minstrels toured America extensively between 1843 and 1855, becoming the most popular minstrel group in the country. They were immortalised in the 1939 film *Swanee River*, in which none other than Al Jolson played Edwin P. Christy.

'Hunky-dory' is thought to have evolved from a New York slang word, 'hunk', meaning 'in a safe position' (as in 'hunker down'), which evolved from the Dutch word *honk*, 'home'. There is another, more colourful but slightly less plausible theory that George Christy picked up the expression from sailors arriving in New York from Japan in the 1850s. The road outside the main gate of the US naval base at Yokosuka in Japan was called Honcho Dori, part of the red-light district. It was here that sailors on leave would go to find girls, alcohol and everything else that was unavailable on board but which would make them feel happy and that all was 'hunky-dory'. It's a nice story, but unconfirmed.

Mumbo-jumbo is nonsense, something with no real meaning. For the origin of this well-known expression we need to go to Africa, and the trips made during the eighteenth century by Western visitors to that continent. One such individual, Francis Moore, an employee of the Royal Africa Company, kept a journal of his time there, published in 1738 as *Travels into the Inland Parts of Africa*, in which he described a 'dreadful bugbear to the women, called Mumbo Jumbo, which is what keeps the women in awe'. This 'bugbear' was a spirit from Mumbo Island in Lake Malawi, thought to have been invented by male tribal leaders in order to keep their women in line. The story goes that, when in-fighting broke out among a man's many wives, he would dress up as Mumbo Jumbo and visit the main culprit in the dead of night, scaring her rigid by shrieking and hollering. The troublemaking missus was then tied to a tree and given an old-fashioned thrashing by the spirit. Clearly he was not to be messed with. The legend travelled back to England with returning missionaries where the word became associated with meaningless rantings of whatever kind.

A load of old **codswallop** is something badly thought out or nonsensical. But does it have anything to do with violent conduct towards fish? In a word: no. 'Wallop' is Australian slang for beer or ale. In 1875, Australian inventor Hiram Codd (1838–87) developed the first bottle with a stopper – a glass marble pushed against a rubber washer to create a seal – that was specially designed to keep sparkling water fizzy until it was opened. As one might expect, Aussie beer drinkers were unimpressed by the new craze for fizzy water, which they regarded as rubbish, and dismissed it as 'Codd's wallop'.

To be full of **blarney** usually means a person is able to talk their way into another's affections, or indeed out of trouble, with considerable ease (see also SCHMOOZE). The word comes from Blarney Castle in County Cork, Ireland, which in 1602 found itself under siege by Elizabeth I's army. The owner, Dermot McCarthy, was trapped inside with his men while the English demanded he surrender his property as a show of loyalty to the queen. But he had no intention of doing so. He also had no intention of slowly starving to death, so he adopted gentle diplomacy as an answer to his problem. After many excuses and much prevarication, including plenty of flattering letters and messages to the queen, the siege eventually failed. Elizabeth was forced to give in to McCarthy's Irish charm and order a withdrawal.

Elizabeth became so frustrated with McCarthy's delaying tactics, however, that she at one point famously exclaimed: 'Odds bodkins! Blarney, Blarney, I will hear no more of this Blarney!' These days, legend has it that if a visitor kisses a certain stone at Blarney Castle – the famous Blarney Stone – they too will be blessed with McCarthy's gift of the gab.

Baloney is a word used primarily in America to describe something that is dubious or nonsensical. In a literal sense, baloney (or 'boloney') is in fact a sausage from the town of Bologna in Italy, which was mass-produced cheaply from the late nineteenth century onwards and introduced to the New World by Italian immigrants. At the time, many people were fairly suspicious of sausages, given that it was almost impossible to tell what was actually in them. The Victorians called them 'little bags of mystery' and generally believed – no doubt quite rightly – that, because they were minced and stuffed, sausages contained the parts of an animal one would rather not look at, let alone eat. Among the growing Italian communities of America's eastern seaboard, however, 'bologna' was a cheap and popular food staple.

The word passed into wider use following a 1930s advertising campaign that used the slogan 'No matter how thin you slice it, it's still baloney', which was soon being used by New Yorkers in response to anything they didn't trust, which included Italians.

Yikes is a word we might use to express fear, alarm or just surprise, an expression that according to the *Oxford English Dictionary* dates back only to 1971. Certainly it was popular among youngsters during the 1970s thanks to its emergence as a catchphrase on the cartoon series *Scooby-Doo*, but other etymologists would argue that the word was in use a number of decades earlier. Around the time of the Second World War, for instance, a 'yike' was a punch-up in London street slang, although any connection between that and 'yikes' is quite tenuous.

Going back even further, however, there is a loose connection between 'yikes' in its current usage and a traditional fox-hunting cry from the later eighteenth century. 'Yoiks' or 'hoiks' was used by hunters to encourage a pack of hounds, and the word is not as obsolete as it may sound: 'huic', pronounced 'hike', is the cry of the modern-day country gentleman as he tally-hoes his way over the landscape, dressed like a circus ringmaster and chasing a fox that he expects to see torn to ribbons by the hounds.

Meanwhile, towards the end of the nineteenth century, 'yoicks' had become a common expression of surprise or alarm, as recorded in a story published in an 1884 edition of the popular *Blackwood's Magazine*, which includes the following: 'With a renewed spirit he climbed into the Hansom Cab and gave the direction. "Yoicks!" he cried, "I am going for it."'

The bars of wood that prevented food, plates and cutlery flying through the air in rough weather (see also FIDDLE) were known as **fiddlesticks**, and it's been suggested that ridiculous games played by sailors using these fiddlesticks led to the quaint exclamation for dismissing something as nonsense. According to another theory, however, the expression derives from folk music, from the sticks or straws used by a second musician to tap out a rhythm on the body of a violin or fiddle as it is being played, hence 'playing fiddlesticks'. But the most likely explanation relates to the actual bow of the violin, or stick with which to play a fiddle (the word deriving from the Latin *vitulari*, 'celebrate a festival', in case you're interested).

The first written reference to the term, used in this sense, may be traced to Shakespeare's *Henry IV, Part 1* (1597), in which young Prince Hal exclaims that 'the devil rides upon a fiddlestick', connecting the commotion that is taking place on stage with the noise the devil might make if he played the violin. Another century would pass before the Irish dramatist George Farquhar premiered his play *Sir Harry Wildair* on London's Drury Lane and had his eponymous character exclaim: 'Golden pleasures! golden fiddlesticks!' The play's popularity is thought to have encouraged the wider use of the word to describe something as inconsequential or mere nonsense.

To **skedaddle** is to leave in a hurry, the word coming to prominence during the American Civil War (1861–5), when it meant 'to run away' or 'to be scattered in a rout'. One theory is that the word may go back to the Greek *skedasis* or 'scattering', which would certainly seem to fit with its modern meaning, but equally it could have taken a different evolutionary route. Prior to its appearance in America, the word had actually been in use in Scotland, meaning 'to spill', often in reference to milk that had slopped from a pail (in the sense that it had escaped), having evolved from the Old Scots word for a watery setting, *skiddle*. The Victorians likewise used a type of sink that they called a 'skiddle'. It is quite likely that this word was merged, probably by Scots migrating to America, with the dialect English *scaddle*, 'to run off in fright'. Which many frontline troops certainly did during the early years of the Civil War – which involved over 100,000 Scots – when faced with a heavily armed professional army.

I can't remember when I last heard the words **toodleloo** or **toodle-pip**, but both are generally thought to have entered the English language during the First World War. They are certainly evocative of a bygone age, in particular the sort of quaint language used by P. G. Wodehouse around that time for his most celebrated characters, Jeeves and Wooster. Indeed, the word appears in Wodehouse's short story 'Jeeves and the Hard Boiled Egg', first published in 1917 and reprinted in *My Man Jeeves* in 1919, in which Bertie Wooster is addressed by his friend Bicky: 'Ripping! I'll be toddling up, then. Toodle-oo, Bertie, old man. See you later.'

According to some etymologists, the origin of this expression, despite seeming the epitome of Englishness, is actually French, having evolved from the phrase *tout à l'heure*, meaning 'see you later'. Which sounds reasonably convincing until you read this excerpt from the popular *Cornhill Magazine*, published in July 1902: 'I tootled down to Cooney's half an hour early.' Here the word 'tootle', a corruption of the much older English word 'toddle' – meaning to walk in an unhurried manner, just as Bicky proposes to do above – and sounding a lot like 'toodle', probably gives us the root of the word occasionally still used today as a cheery goodbye. Yet another theory suggests the word, especially in the form 'toodle-pip', was an echo of the newly invented car horn, 'toot toot, pip pip', but that seems highly suspect to me.

TRADE AND INDUSTRY

Spondulics is a slang word for money, used mainly in the south of England. The *Oxford English Dictionary* explains that it is a word of 'fanciful origin', which doesn't tell us much. My Greek friends have traced it back to classical times and the word *spondulikos*, which evolved from *spondulos*, a type of seashell that was supposedly once used as a form of currency throughout the ancient world. A second Greek connection comes from the word *spondylo*, 'spine', applied figuratively to money on the basis that a stack of coins resembles the column of vertebrae in the spine. It may sound far-fetched but the connection had clearly been made by 1867, the year in which John Mitchell Bonnell, in his book *A Manual of the Art of Prose Composition*, defined 'spondulics' as a 'coin pile, ready for counting'.

I have heard many explanations for the origin of the word **quid**, a slang word for the British pound coin, formerly pound note. These range from the ludicrous – English fishermen used to trade in squids – to the curious: American frontiersmen traded in units of chewing tobacco known as quids. There is the dubious story about Gaelic-speaking soldiers in the British army demanding *mo chuid*, 'my money', and then the slightly more believable, but still unlikely, link to the Latin term *quid pro quo*, a commonly used expression meaning 'a more or less equal exchange'.

But I have a better explanation for you. Another story I have heard concerns the Royal Paper Mill, once located at Quidhampton in Wiltshire, which used to provide the special paper for all of the banknotes commissioned by the Royal Mint, leading to the NICKNAME for the pound note. But since the only reference I can find to Quidhampton Mill in Wiltshire is connected to that particular story, with details remaining conspicuously absent from local government records, it probably didn't exist.

Instead the records led me to a Quidhampton Water Mill, which operated for 700 years between the thirteenth and mid-twentieth centuries, and was used for fulling locally produced worsted cloth. But in the process of finding all this out, I accidentally discovered the Overton Paper Mill, formerly called the Quidhampton Paper Mill, which lay between the villages of Overton and Quidhampton to the west of Basingstoke in Hampshire, another county altogether.

It appears that this was the mill that produced the special banknote paper used by the Royal Mint, along with other banknote printers around the world, and did so for several centuries.

In attempting to dispel a myth, it seems I have accidentally confirmed it. With apologies to the good folk of Quidhampton in Wiltshire – it looks as if it wasn't your mill after all.

In America the equivalent smallest note of currency, the dollar, has its own NICKNAME: a **buck**. The term comes from poker playing. Back in the days of the Wild West, the most common knife available was known as a buckhorn knife, so called because the handle was carved from the horn of a buck deer. As all cowboys and ranchers carried them around, one of these knives would always be placed in front of whoever was due to deal the next hand in a game of poker. Later, at the great casinos and gaming houses in Las Vegas, a silver dollar was used in place of a knife, and that is how the slang term for the currency arose.

In poker games where the stakes were running too high for a player, he could opt out of his turn at dealing by passing the buckhorn knife (or buck) to the next player. Even if he chose to play, he still avoided the responsibility of setting the bets next time around by **passing the buck** along. This expression was known by 1865 and the first recorded use was by Mark Twain in 1872. In 1945, President Truman famously had a plaque made for his desk in the

Oval Office, which read **The Buck Stops Here**, a clear declaration that he was prepared to accept responsibility for all the decisions taken during his term of office. Later presidents Carter, Ford and Nixon all copied the idea, and the expression has since been widely used.

For such a simple and familiar-looking object, the **piggybank** has a rather uncertain history. The most likely theory for its derivation is that the word has nothing to do with pigs and everything to do with a kind of orange clay, called 'pygg clay', used for making pottery and storage jars in the Middle Ages. Anybody could make a pygg jar by simply gathering the wet clay, shaping it by hand and leaving it by a fire until it dried and hardened. As a result, pygg jars were very much household items by the fifteenth century, coinciding with a move away from bartering to a notable increase in the use of coins for payment and trade. In the centuries before simple country folk so much as clapped eyes on a **bank**, hardworking labourers and craftsmen could hide or bury their groats in sealed pygg jars. And that's how 'pygg banks', as they were known by the early eighteenth century, became a traditional means for saving small amounts of cash.

Pigs aside, the word 'bank', in a financial sense, evolved from the Italian *banco*, meaning 'bench', and it has an interesting history. In medieval Venice, once the centre of world trade, dealers would set up benches or counters in the main squares at which they conducted trade with visitors to the city from various nations, all with their different currencies. These men were universally trusted and relied upon, and traders could borrow, exchange and even leave money with them while they continued on their travels. The currency would be traded with other individuals, earning a nice bit of interest in the process, and traders could return to collect even larger sums than they had left behind. This system was an early form of world banking, with the trustworthy Venetians regarded very much as people who could be **banked upon** (as well as with).

A **fire sale**, a sale in which a company sells off its entire stock at heavily discounted prices, is generally thought to have become part of the English language in 1895, after a fire at a bookshop called Whitcombe & Tombs in Dunedin, New Zealand, led to the first advertised 'fire sale' of surviving but damaged stock. But although Whitcombe & Tombs did exist – and still does, as Whitcoulls, one of the largest book retailers on the islands – there is no record in its company history of the famous fire.

For the likelier origin of the term, we need to turn to Fitchburg, the third-largest city in Worcester County, Massachusetts, and this account in the records of its History Society:

In December 1856, the account of an extensive fire in the American House mentions the following occupants: E. B. Gee, clothing; T. B. Choate, drugs; J. C. Tenny, boots and shoes; Maraton Upton, dry goods; and M. W. Hayward, groceries. Maraton Upton has removed his stock to No. 9 Rollstock Block, and advertised 'Extraordinary Fire Sale; customers are invited to call and examine the goods which are still warm.'

Maraton Upton's fire sale clearly pre-dates the supposed Whitcombe & Tombs event by nearly forty years. And the American connection makes greater sense given the modern use of the word in reference to the sale of Major League sports stars at the end of a season.

To be on **tenterhooks** is to be anxious or under stress while waiting for something specific to happen. One popular theory is that the word stems from tent hooks, which are used to keep a canvas tense and therefore watertight, but its real origin is related to industry rather than camping. In bygone days, workers at the great mills would attach newly produced cloth to hooks and stretch it across large frames known as 'tenters', from the Latin *tendere*, 'to stretch out'. Anything, or anyone, strained into a state of tension was subsequently described as being 'on tenterhooks'.

A **jalopy** is a beaten-up old wreck of a car, or any other worn-out piece of machinery. The definitive origin of this unusual word is unknown, although it was first noted in 1924 as American slang and then widely used during the 1930s when the market for second-hand cars was beginning to establish itself. The 1934 edition of *Webster's New International Dictionary* reads: 'Jaloppi: a cheap make of automobile, an automobile only fit for junking', and the term was later popularised by Jack Kerouac's seminal novel *On the Road* (1957). From the late 1920s onwards, fictional amateur detectives the Hardy Boys also used jalopies as transport.

The word is thought to have been coined in the early 1920s by New Orleans dockworkers, who were known to call old cars that were heading for the scrap-metal yards of Xalapa in Mexico 'jalopies', because the name of their destination, which is pronounced 'Jalapa', was stamped on the side of each vehicle. It wasn't long before 'jalopy', meaning 'bound for Xalapa', had passed over into everyday American English. Incidentally, the same town is also known for its world-famous jalapeño pepper, providing an unexpected link between a clapped-out old banger and your favourite chilli popper.

Navvies is a word we use for builders, labourers or anybody else engaged in unskilled manual work. During the nineteenth century, as plans to expand Britain's infrastructure grew more advanced and more ambitious, the demand for cheap labour – to dig canals, build roads and enlarge the railway network – became ever greater. In Ireland, on the other hand, there was no work and no food and everybody was either starving to death or leaving for America. Those who didn't headed east to England, where anybody with a pick or shovel could find enough work to feed his family back on the Emerald Isle.

The Irish labourers were perfect for this itinerant work: unlike British workers, who wanted to stay close to their families, the Irish were already far from home and it didn't really matter where they found themselves. After all, if you are building the London to Birmingham canal and you start off in London, you are eventually going to end up in

Birmingham. Since southern labourers didn't particularly want to go to Birmingham – and were not quite as desperate for work – it fell to the Irish to build the Victorian navigation network of canals, roads and railways, which is how they became known as 'navvies' (navigators).

Something performed in a **slapdash** manner is done in a hurry and without due care and attention, usually leading to a poor result and, in my case, having to get somebody else to do it properly. In the seventeenth century, slapdash was a common plastering technique whereby mortar would be 'slapped' against a wall and then 'dashed' with a trowel to smooth the finish. Basically it was a way of rough-plastering a wall, similar to roughcast or pebbledash, and at one time commonly known as a 'slap and dash' finish throughout the building trade. (See also SLAP-BANG.)

Spick and **span** are two words we only ever use as a pair, to describe something as tidy and clean. In America the expression is particularly well known thanks to a major household-cleaning product called Spic and Span, which appeared in 1933 and continues to be sold to this day. But the words have nothing to do with either 'Hi**span**ic' or '**Span**ish', as some of our cousins across the water – presumably those with South American cleaners – appear to believe.

The expression was in use as far back as 1665, when Samuel Pepys commented in his diary that 'My Lady Batten was walking along the dirty lane with spick and span white shoes.' In those days, it was generally used in the form 'spick and span new', meaning 'brand new', and therefore perhaps also related to the phrase 'brand spanking new'. 'Span', in the form 'span new', is believed to have evolved from the Norse *spán-nýr*, literally 'chip new' – that is, as new as a freshly cut wooden chip – while 'spick' was a later addition, taken from the Dutch *spiksplinternieuw*, 'splinter new'.

In the sixteenth century, a **knacker** was a harness maker, the word having most likely been inspired by the many 'knacks' (an obsolete word akin to the more modern 'knick-knacks') that make up a harness. By the seventeenth century, however, knackers had become responsible for all animals that were not fit for human consumption – the butcher would deal with the rest – including cats and dogs, and horses that were no longer able to work. These would be sent to the 'knacker' to be made into something more useful, such as glue. He might also be required to castrate animals, which explains the slang term for testicles (see also AVOCADO, BOLLOCKS).

Knackers' yards, known collectively as 'the knackeries', are defined by the Slaughter House Act of 1974 as 'a premises used in connection with the business of slaughtering, skinning and cutting up of animals whose flesh is not intended for human consumption'. Without a doubt, any tired old horse heading that way is well and truly **knackered**.

FASHION STATEMENTS

Bloomers are a big old pair of lady's pants that are worn more for comfort than for sex appeal, especially the baggy ones. But, believe it or not, there was a time when a pair of bloomers was considered high fashion.

Bloomers were invented in the mid-nineteenth century by Elizabeth Smith Miller (1822–1911) of New York state, with the intention of preserving a lady's modesty while engaged in activities such as horse riding and cycling. Worn below the skirt, these pantaloons were long baggy pants, based on traditional Turkish trousers, which narrowed to a cuff at the ankle. They took a while to catch on and were widely ridiculed by the press, although when prominent women's rights campaigner Amelia Jenks Bloomer (1818–94) started wearing them in the early 1850s, bloomers – as they became known after she enthused about them in her magazine *The Lily* – grew in popularity.

On a related note, the **Suffragettes** took their name from the word 'suffrage', 'the right to vote', which comes from the Latin *suffragium*, 'voting tablet'.

The humble **bikini**, one of the great inventions of modern times, has aroused much debate, among other things, over the course of its short history.

The origin of the two-piece swimsuit can be traced back much further, however, to a mosaic from Sicily dating from AD 280–300 and depicting ten women exercising in what we would now call bikinis. But an austere few centuries followed; indeed, even as recently as 1910 a woman could be arrested in America for wearing a one-piece swimsuit on the beach. The introduction of women's swimming at the 1912 Olympics in Stockholm changed attitudes to women's beachwear, although it is amusing to note that no female American swimmers actually competed since team rules forbade ladies from participating in anything skimpier than a skirt. Quite ironic, really, given that it was Hollywood stars such as Audrey Hepburn, Vivien Leigh and Ava Gardner who set pulses racing around the world only a few decades later by being pictured in tiny two-piece numbers.

By the end of the Second World War, two-piece swimwear had become so popular that a French engineer named Louis Réard (1897–1984), who was running his mother's lingerie boutique (I know, I know: the words 'mother' and 'lingerie' should never appear together in the same sentence) near Paris, designed a costume that he advertised as the 'smallest bathing suit in the world'. It is an indication of the era, however, that the bottom half still covered the navel. What would Jordan make of that? (No, not the country.)

Réard's final design, refined to reveal the navel, was deemed so racy that he was unable to find a girl to model it for him when he launched the costume in 1946; he had to hire Micheline Bernardini, a nineteen-year-old nude dancer from the Casino de Paris. Just a few days beforehand, the American military had begun testing a new series of nuclear weapons at a small group of uninhabited Micronesian islands deep in the Pacific Ocean, and suddenly 'Bikini Atoll' was big news across the world. Some historians have claimed that the two islands of Bikini Atoll were similar in shape to Réard's design, hence the name, but in fact the Frenchman deliberately called his costume the 'bikini' to suggest the explosive effect they were about to have on the men of the Western world.

Luckily the Americans weren't testing on the nearby Eschsholtz or Rongerik Atolls, as neither name has quite the same ring to it. The native islanders who were relocated prior to the nuclear testing had always called the land 'Pikini', meaning 'land of the coconuts' in Marshallese, although that's not the reason why bikinis and coconuts go together in the minds of teenage boys.

The classic **blazer** is a short, blue, double-breasted jacket with brass buttons and an obvious association with military tradition. The popular story of its origin is that the commanding officer of the frigate HMS *Blazer* dressed his crew in short blue and white striped jackets for a formal visit by Queen Victoria in 1845. Her Majesty was impressed, and their popularity subsequently spread throughout the navy, with other crews issued their own individually styled 'blazers'.

Blazers are nowadays more closely associated with sporting clubs than the military, and indeed it is a venerable old sporting association that holds the rival claim for the origin of the word. The prestigious Lady Margaret Boat Club of St John's College, Cambridge, was formed in 1825, and its members claim that their distinctive, bright-scarlet jackets inspired the NICKNAME 'blazers' (see BLAZE in its second sense). This claim naturally casts doubt on the crew of HMS *Blazer* and their pioneering jackets. There certainly was an HMS *Blazer*, a sloop that surveyed the east coast of England under Captain John Washington in the 1840s, but it was small and unlikely to have been boarded by Queen Victoria. Furthermore, there is no mention of the origin of the blazer in the boat's official history. So perhaps the bright 'blazers' of the Lady Margaret Boat Club, which incidentally was one of the founding teams of the Oxford and Cambridge Boat Race in 1829, win the day after all.

Jodhpurs are a pair of riding breeches that are designed to be tight around the waist, loose and flared along the thigh, and then tapered back into a tight fit between the knee and ankle. Their design was copied from a traditional northern Indian trouser commonly worn in Rajasthan during the days of the British Raj, when **polo** – essentially hockey played on horseback – was taken up with great enthusiasm by the British. (Developed originally in Persia, where it was played from the fifth century BC, the game then spread to other parts of Asia, including the Indian subcontinent – where it was known by various names, including *pulu*, the word for the wooden ball used by the players.)

One particularly keen polo player was Sir Pratap Singh, the youngest son of the Maharaja of Jodhpur – the capital of Rajasthan – who had adapted the standard British style of trouser to taper at the calf, rather like the traditional Indian garment, so that it could be worn with riding boots. When he was invited to England for Queen Victoria's Diamond Jubilee celebrations in 1897, Singh brought his entire polo team with him and toured the country playing exhibition matches, winning regularly enough to cause a sensation. The team's success, coupled with their exotic looks, led to tailors all over the country designing their own versions of these breeches from Jodhpur, which became an instant hit within fashionable society.

A **cardigan** is a jacket made of wool, with buttons up the front. But I am hoping you already knew that. Back in the 1850s, when the British were engaged in their favourite pastime of that century, war (this time with Russia), British troops stationed in Crimea were subjected to spectacularly long and brutal winters. But they were an enterprising lot, the British. One of them, James Thomas Brudenell (1797–1868), who led the cavalry during the notoriously stupid Charge of the Light Brigade on 25 October 1854, arranged for a thick woollen vest with long sleeves and 'buttons like a shirt' to be knitted for him. The idea quickly spread through the ranks and file and suddenly Brudenell, aka the Earl of Cardigan, had inadvertently invented the garment favoured by golfers and granddads the world over.

Although Cardigan led the ill-fated Charge, he was under the command of Lieutenant-General George Charles Bingham, the 3rd Earl of Lucan (1800–1888), the less-than-illustrious ancestor of the rather more notorious 7th Earl of Lucan, wanted by the police since 1974 and quite possibly hiding in the back of your garden shed.

The Charge of the Light Brigade took place during the infamous Battle of **Balaclava**, so named after the port in southern Ukraine that also gave its name to the woollen helmet my nan knitted and forced me to wear to school in winter. Staying with the Crimean War, and for the fashionistas among you, the **raglan** overcoat was designed and worn throughout the campaign by Fitzroy James Henry

Somerset (1788–1855), also known as the 1st Baron Raglan. The style of coat has all but passed into obscurity these days but the **raglan sleeve** – extending in one piece to the collar, perhaps originally to create the best fit for the arm Raglan lost at the Battle of Waterloo – remains a well-known design throughout the fashion industry. Apparently. (For other war-related items of clothing, see BLÜCHERS.)

A **tattoo** can be one of two things: either an outdoor military display or a pattern of indelible ink somewhere on the body. There is no connection between the two definitions other than that they share exactly the same word, which suggests they must have two unconnected origins.

Military tattoos, such as the world-famous Edinburgh Tattoo, can be traced to the Dutch word *taptoe*, which, when used in English military parlance, meant 'turn off the taps' – in other words, 'stop drinking and get back to the barracks'. Dating from the seventeenth century when the British army was fighting in the Netherlands, the term was applied to the procedure whereby drummers would be sent out from the garrison at night to signal the curfew to those soldiers out drinking in the local taverns. Over time the drumming was performed just for show, evolving into the elaborate displays that take place today.

Skin designs are a completely different thing, of course, and were first seen by Western eyes when Captain James Cook voyaged into the unknown in the 1760s. He and his crew discovered many small and previously undiscovered islands in the southern ocean, including Tahiti, Samoa, New Zealand and the southern continent now called Australia. When they first stopped in Tahiti, the crew received a friendly welcome. Observing their hosts, Joseph Banks, the scientist aboard Cook's flagship HMS *Endeavour*, referred in his journal to the variety of body markings on display: 'the way the people mark themselves indelibly, each of them is so marked by their humour or disposition'. Many of the crew allowed themselves to be 'marked' by the native artists – adopting the Tahitian word for 'mark', *tatau* – and thereby beginning the long association between sailors and body art.

Sideburns, or whiskers on the side of a man's face, have gone in and out of fashion for years, having made their most recent appearance back in the late 1960s thanks to the Beatles' iconic album cover for *Sgt. Pepper's Lonely Hearts Club Band*, after which it seemed every man in England was proudly sporting them.

While side whiskers have been worn by men for centuries – Alexander the Great, for instance, is depicted with them in a mosaic from Pompeii – the word itself is much more recent, dating back to the mid-nineteenth century and a certain General Ambrose Everett Burnside (1824–81). Having served without distinction during the American Civil War (1861–5), leading his regiment to disastrous defeat at the Battle of Fredericksburg in 1862, Burnside was lucky enough to end up on the winning side and went on to become Governor of Rhode Island. During his high-profile political career, Burnside was regarded as a popular character and especially noted for his distinctive facial hair: two huge bushy sets of side whiskers ran from his ears to his moustache while his chin and neck remained clean-shaven. The New York press coined the word 'burnsides' to describe this flamboyant style, the words 'burn' and 'side' becoming reversed over time to give us the modern-day expression.

In his work on the American Civil War, *Mr Lincoln's Army* (1951), historian Bruce Catton describes Burnside as: 'Physically impressive, tall, a little stout and wearing what was probably the most artistic and awe-inspiring set of whiskers in all of that bewhiskered army.' A statue of Ambrose Burnside, erected after his sudden death in 1881 and featuring those awe-inspiring sideburns, can be found in the centre of Burnside Park in Providence, Rhode Island.

It is thanks to Prussian Field Marshal Gebhard Leberecht von Blücher (1742–1819), and his concern about the quality of his army's footwear during the Napoleonic Wars, that we can add **blüchers** to the surprisingly long list of fashion items inspired by warfare. Blüchers, an avant-garde style of lace-up shoe 200 years ago, evolved into what became known as **oxfords** when students at Oxford University adopted the style of shoe worn by returning soldiers.

Something that is generally not well recorded by history is that the Iron Duke, the Duke of **Wellington** (1769–1852), namesake not only of a style of boot distributed to his troops but also of a certain dish made of beef wrapped in pastry, was actually losing the Battle of Waterloo to Napoleon until the timely intervention of Blücher. So it is worth noting that if it hadn't been for Blücher, the students of Oxford would not have had their famous shoe. And they would probably also be speaking French.

A **belvedere** is a structure at the top of a building from which one has a view over rolling hills or a beautiful panorama. For much of human history, however, surveying the countryside from on high has not been something done for leisure, but rather for military purposes. Lookouts would keep watch near towns and the coast, and alert people to any unexpected approach, whether a triumphant returning army or a battle-ready approaching enemy. But from the late fifteenth century onwards, it gradually became quite fashionable just to enjoy a view for its own sake.

The word 'belvedere', meaning 'beautiful view', comes from the Italian *bel* ('beautiful') and *vedere* ('to see'). The first belvedere was a summerhouse by the same name that was built for Pope Innocent VIII in the 1480s. The architect Donato Bramante was later commissioned to design a vast courtyard, the Cortile del Belvedere, to link the Villa Belvedere with the Vatican. An ancient Roman statue of Apollo, rediscovered in 1489, was put in a prime position in the courtyard and subsequently became known as the *Apollo Belvedere*.

The fashion for belvederes spread the world over and there are now very few English-speaking cities without a hotel called 'The Belvedere'. If ever you happen to stay in one and don't have a room with a view, you can be pretty sure you've been DIDDLED.

In 1849, the London milliners Thomas and William **Bowler** took an order from the firm of hatters Locke & Co., who had been commissioned to produce a tight-fitting, low-crowned, strong hat to protect gamekeepers from being hit on the head by either branches or angry poachers.

Previously they had worn top hats that were easy to knock off in a struggle and offered no protection at all. The new hat was in effect designed to act as a lightweight helmet.

When the buyer, a British politician and soldier named Edward Keppel Coke, arrived to collect the new hats, he is said to have placed one on the floor and jumped on it to test its strength. Confident that it could hold his weight, he paid the bill and the new **coke hat** went into production. In a somewhat modified form, the coke hat was soon being exported all over the British Empire after being renamed in honour of the brothers who had designed it. Except in the United States, that is, where it is known as a **derby**, due to an association with horse racing, although the term is also applied to the fancy hats worn by women at the Kentucky Derby – a US version of Ascot.

Jeans, the iconic denim trousers that never seem to go out of fashion, are believed to have been invented by Levi Strauss (1829–1902), a German immigrant to America whose wholesale business supplied clothes to the gold miners and cattle ranchers of the Old West. Strauss recognised that workers needed something tough and durable to wear, and in 1873 began manufacturing denim trousers that he simply called Levi's, after his own name.

Strauss was familiar with the hard-wearing trousers that had been worn by European sailors since the sixteenth and seventeenth centuries. The material was first developed near Turin and was then commissioned by the independent Republic of Genoa, an important naval and trading province, for the Genoese navy, which required all-purpose trousers for the hard life at sea. Sailors would wash them by dragging them behind their ships in nets and leaving them out on the deck to dry. Believe it or not, the word 'jeans' is derived from 'Genoa', the first city in which they created a fashion craze. **Denim**, a similarly durable material now synonymous with 'jeans', originally came from Nîmes (*de Nîmes*).

The adoption of jeans as a statement of youth and coolness didn't happen until the 1950s, when they were most famously sported by the ultimate 'rebel without an airbag', the equally iconic James Dean.

CRIMES AND MISDEMEANOURS

Bamboozle – in the sense of 'to confuse and take advantage of' – first appeared in print in the early eighteenth century, and was in regular enough use for it to be included in an article penned in 1712 for the *Tatler* magazine by Jonathan Swift – the author, among other satirical writings, of *Gulliver's Travels* (1726) – which was rather loftily entitled 'A Proposal for Correcting, Improving, and Ascertaining the English Tongue'.

Some lazy etymologists have in the past attempted to connect the words 'bamboo' and BOOZE to suggest that anybody drinking enough of a certain bamboo-based concoction was likely to become confused and bewildered, leading to the origin of this colourful expression. The *Oxford Dictionary of Word Histories*, on the other hand, claims the word first appeared around 1700, having evolved from the old Scottish word *bombaze* or *bumbaze*, meaning 'to confound or confuse' (see also BEFUDDLED). It sounds more plausible, but personally I prefer the idea of it being the result of getting SOZZLED on bamboo liquor.

The sort of young criminal dispatched to BORSTAL might have been called a **ruffian** in times past (see also HOODLUM, LARRIKIN, THUG, YAHOO). Although the term sounds as if it should have evolved from 'rough', there is no connection between the two words. Charles Dickens was quite forceful on this point, as is clear from 'The Ruffian', one of the articles collected in *The Uncommercial Traveller* (1861):'I entertain so strong an objection to the euphonious softening of ruffian into rough, which has lately become popular, that I restore the right word to the heading of this paper.'

In the mid–eighteenth century, Samuel Johnson defined 'ruffian' in his dictionary as a robber or a cut–throat murderer. The word, thought to have evolved from the Italian *ruffiano*, meaning 'pimp', appears to have been popularised earlier that century by the Freemasons in the story 'Three Ruffians, Supposed to be Three Fellow-Craft', first published in the book *Masonry Dissected* in 1730. According to the story, these ruffians were engaged in infiltrating the secret society to gain access to sensitive information, such as silly handshakes and so forth.

Jiggery-pokery is a wonderful English word used in reference to somebody who is skulking around, behaving in an underhand and deceitful manner and generally up to no good (see also SKULDUGGERY). Which, according to our English ancestors, was a pretty apt description of the Scottish. The word evolved from the old Scots expression 'joukery-pawkery', meaning 'to dodge and deceive'. More recently, jiggery-pokery appeared as one of the three made-up spells Harry Potter used in his attempt to frighten away his Muggle cousin Dudley Dursley in *Harry Potter and the Chamber of Secrets* (1998).

The word **Ponzi** came to worldwide attention in 2008 when American conman Bernard Madoff was arrested for using his lucrative investment company as a front for a **Ponzi scheme** – a fraudulent investment operation funded almost solely by money from its investors rather than any genuine enterprise. For many years Bernard L. Madoff Investment Securities LLC had been attracting investors from all over the world by promising, and delivering, higher returns on investments than any other institution could match. It was eventually revealed, however, that Madoff had invested very little and simply paid high rates of return to earlier investors using the money paid by new clients – who, in turn, would later receive high returns from newer clients. It was a house of cards that could never remain standing. Although Madoff's scam continued undetected for over fifteen years, billions of dollars were ultimately lost and a number of its victims were driven to suicide. Madoff will now spend the next 150 years securely in prison.

The original Ponzi after whom all this is named went down in history as one of the great swindlers of all time. Charles Ponzi (1882–1949) operated the same kind of investment fraud in New York in 1920, quickly attracting $450,000 in business (worth $5 million in 2011). By July of that year, people were re-mortgaging their homes to invest in Ponzi's incredible investment scheme. But a suspicious and intrepid journalist working at the *Boston Post* eventually revealed the scam, winning the Pulitzer Prize for investigative journalism in the process, and Charles Ponzi's fall from grace was as swift and spectacular as his rise to fame. After spending fourteen years in jail, he was deported to Brazil, where he wrote his autobiography but died in poverty in 1949, having suffered a brain haemorrhage.

Although Charles Ponzi ran the highest-profile Ponzi scheme the world had ever known, the wily Italian was not the first person to scam Americans with a Ponzi-style investment fraud. That dubious honour most likely goes to an accountant called William F. Miller, who in 1899 used the same system to steal $1 million. Further research, however, reveals that Charles Dickens describes exactly the same form of investment fraud in his 1857 novel *Little Dorrit*, in which the Dorrit family are unwittingly lured to financial collapse. As it is unlikely that Dickens simply made it up himself, it is quite possible that greedy investors have been falling for the Ponzi scam for at least 200 years and, I am sure, will continue to succumb in the future.

An **eavesdropper** is someone who deliberately tries to overhear what someone else is saying, without being detected. But what has this activity to do with eaves or indeed dropping? Centuries ago, houses in Britain had no gutters or drainpipes; instead the roof extended well beyond the walls of the building, enabling rainwater to drip to the ground away from the house. The area between the edge of the roof and the walls was known originally as the 'eavesdrip' and latterly the 'eavesdrop'. The eavesdrop also served as a shelter for passers-by, who would stay close to the walls of a building in order to keep out of the rain, but this position also enabled them to overhear conversations going on inside the house. Those who lingered longer than necessary hence became known as 'eavesdroppers'.

To **blackmail** somebody is to demand money by threatening to do something harmful to them – usually to expose their secrets. Perhaps surprisingly, given the word's common usage in the corridors of power, it originated in the Highlands of Scotland in the seventeenth century. The 'mail' part of it is an old Scottish word for 'rent', usually spelt either *maill* or *male*, and related to the Old Norse *mal*, 'agreement or contract'. Scottish tenants traditionally paid their rent in what was known as 'white money' – silver coins – but in the seventeenth century certain clan chiefs began a protection racket, threatening farmers and traders with violence if they didn't pay to be protected from other clans. This informal new kind of rent soon became known as 'black money' or 'black rent', hence 'blackmail', and it gradually took on a more general meaning for the practice of obtaining money by threat of violence.

During the twentieth century, the art of demanding money to 'protect' somebody's secrets was honed and the use of the word 'blackmail' extended to describe this. Blackmail was not specifically criminalised in the UK until 1968.

If someone is described as being on the **fiddle**, it implies they are involved in something not entirely within the rules, and perhaps gaining more than they should from it. As unlikely as it may seem, this is in fact a nautical saying, related to the square-shaped dinner plates (of 'square meal' fame) traditionally used by sailors on the high seas. These square plates, rather like the tables themselves (see FIDDLESTICKS), had a raised rim called a fiddle, which prevented food falling off while the ship rolled from side to side. Crew members would be mistrustful of a fellow sailor with so much food that it piled up against the rim of his plate, and he would be regarded as 'on the fiddle': taking or being given more than his due. (See also DIDDLED.)

An **assassin** is a paid mercenary, usually someone who kills a powerful or important figure for what he considers to be a just cause (i.e. his own). Historically, the assassins were a group of Muslim fanatics who defended the Holy Land from the Christian Crusaders in around AD 1090. They were led by Hasan-e Sabbah, a Persian missionary who enthusiastically established his own murderous credentials by dispatching several high-profile Muslim leaders over the next two decades.

115

The assassins' main targets were members of the ruling Seljuk authority, who controlled vast areas of what was once the Persian Empire and had extended their dominion into Syria by the twelfth century. Living in remote areas in the mountains, Sabbah's followers would identify a single target and send in one or two men to commit a violent attack, usually having fuelled themselves with their drug of choice, hashish. This is how they became known, and feared, as the *Hashashshin* or 'Hashish Eaters'.

The original story behind this practice was told by Marco Polo in an account of his travels to the East in 1298. Polo wrote of the 'Old Man of the Mountain' (Sabbah, in other words) who kept boys as young as twelve at his fortress hideaway, with the intention of training them to become fearless warriors. The boys would be given hashish and, after passing out, they would be taken to a garden of tranquil beauty, where they would awake to find themselves surrounded by lovely maidens who would entertain them in any way they pleased. After a few days, the Old Man would reappear and explain that they had been given a glimpse of the paradise that awaited them if they followed his instructions to the letter and were willing to die in the process. This was considered an innovative and effective tactic at a time when the art of warfare generally consisted of nothing subtler than a slugging match between two armies. The *Hashashshin*, however, remained hidden and appeared to be normal members of a community until the opportunity to strike presented itself. Sounds a little familiar, doesn't it?

A **hoodlum** is a street hooligan or a RUFFIAN, and quite possibly a gangster (see also LARRIKIN, THUG, YAHOO). The word was first used in print in San Francisco in 1875, after which it quickly spread across America. But where had it come from?

In the mid-nineteenth century, Chinese immigration to the West Coast of the New World was on the rise, thanks both to the Opium Wars between China and Britain and to the Californian Gold Rush. But the German and Irish settlers who were already well established, and perceived themselves as having done most of the 'hard work', resented this new influx of what amounted to cheap labour. This, coupled with the fact their new neighbours were not pasty-faced northern Europeans like themselves, resulted in a very frosty welcome for the Chinese. But simple racism wasn't the heart of the problem. The issue was that most Chinese immigrants, unlike the established settlers who were by now a couple of generations into American life, did not try to integrate. Instead of buying land, building farms and forming new communities, many Chinese arrived on their own without their families, worked as labourers, selling their food and even their women, and then left, returning to China with whatever wealth they had managed to accumulate, only to be replaced by a new wave of immigrants.

Congress soon put a stop to this by passing the Chinese Exclusion Act of 1882, prohibiting any immigration from China for ten years, after which the act was extended. But this was not before gangs of idle 'hoodlums', white youths of German or Irish descent, had begun a campaign of harassment directed at the Chinese who were already in the country. The problem was described by journalist Samuel Williams in his article 'The City of the Golden Gate', published in an edition of *Scribner's Monthly* in 1875: 'The Hoodlum is a distinctive San Francisco product. He drinks, gambles, steals, runs after lewd women and sets buildings on fire. One of his chief diversions, when he is in a more pleasant mood, is stoning Chinamen. That the Hoodlum appeared only three or four years ago is somewhat alarming.'

Barrère and Leland's *Dictionary of Slang, Jargon and Cant* of 1889 suggests that 'hoodlum' is linked to 'hood lahnt', which apparently meant 'lazy mandarin' in pidgin English, although I have not been able to trace the word 'lahnt' to anything at all. Other etymologists, meanwhile, claim that the word derives from 'Muldoon', the name of the feared leader of a gang of ruffians which was spelt backwards, 'Noodlum', by a journalist in his article on the gang, in order to prevent reprisals. Over time – owing to a series of Chinese whispers, no doubt – the name became 'hoodlum'. But I prefer the explanation offered by the wonderfully named Dr J. T. Krumpelman, who explained in 1935 that, as German immigrants comprised by far the largest ethnic group in San Francisco at the time (see DUDE), the word 'hoodlum' must have evolved from the Bavarian *hodalump*, which translates as 'good for nothing' or RAGAMUFFIN.

Shenanigans can be either high-spirited mischief (see TOMFOOLERY) or a more dishonest activity altogether, depending on the context in which it is used. There are several suggestions for the origin of this strange word. One, put forward by a 1948 edition of the quarterly academic journal *American Speech*, argues that it evolved from a German word for a nail that holds the metal rim to a wooden wheel, *Schinagel*, which in turn leads to a German slang word, *schinageln*, meaning 'to work', as well as *Schenigelei*, 'trick'. Although I have a word for this theory too: POPPYCOCK.

I also don't go in for the theory that the Spanish word *chanchada*, meaning 'dirty trick', is the root we are looking for. To me, 'shenanigans' sounds distinctly Irish. We know the word was first recorded in San Francisco's *Town Talk* newspaper in April 1855, and we also know that nearly 2 million Irish men, women and children migrated to the New World during the Potato Famine of 1845–52. Many of them headed straight to California, where the Gold Rush was in full swing. With evidence like this, it is hardly surprising that an Irish word could have ended up in San Francisco by 1855, and we don't have to search too hard for its origin either: the Gaelic word playing tricks is *sionnachuighm*, pronounced 'shinnuckeem', which may be literally translated as 'I play the fox'. That sounds far more plausible to me than little German nails.

Bootleggers are petty criminals who sell items, traditionally alcohol, without proper permission. By avoiding tax or other duties, they can undercut the rest of the market, making their wares cheaper and therefore more in demand. Nowadays bootleggers are better known for making illegal copies of music or films and selling them without paying the royalties properly due.

The expression was first recorded in the mid-nineteenth century in America, in reference to traders who sold illegal liquor to the Native American communities in the Far West. They would ride out to the reservations with hipflasks of alcohol concealed in their riding boots, as a result of which they became known to the authorities as 'bootleggers'. Travelling across the country and over the pond to the UK, the phrase was soon applied to anyone involved in counterfeiting or the illegal distribution of goods, particularly associated with the Prohibition era of the 1920s during which bootleggers could make huge profits from the sale of illicitly produced alcohol (see HOOCH).

A **henchman** used to be any solid and strong supporter of a person of rank. In modern times, henchmen tend to be dubious sidekicks who carry out unpleasant duties

120

for their employer, generally by intimidation, either verbal or physical (see also BOUNCERS).

The original 'henchmen' were stable staff or horse grooms. The word evolved from the Old English word *hengest*, which, around the fourteenth century, meant 'male horse' or 'stallion'. 'Henxmen', as they were known by the later Middle Ages, were a common feature of noble households and royal courts; by the reign of Elizabeth I, the royal henchmen would walk or ride alongside their sovereign or master during parades and processions.

For such a small word, generally used to describe small people, **thug** (see also HOODLUM, LARRIKIN, RUFFIAN, YAHOO) has a rich and colourful history. By no means a modern concept, **thuggery** can in fact be traced back over thousands of years.

In India, *thuggee*, which is related to the Hindi *thag*, 'thief', and the Sanskrit *sthaga*, 'cunning' or 'dishonest', is the ruthless highway robbery of merchants and pilgrims travelling across the country. During the golden age of thuggery, career bandits – or Thugs, as they were known – developed a way of joining a travelling caravan, and in some cases journeyed for hundreds of miles in order to earn the trust and respect of a group. For attacks on some of the larger, better-defended caravans, the Thugs would infiltrate the group at pre-arranged intervals, pretending not to know one another. But later, once a camp had been set up in some remote area and the travellers were noisily going about their evening preparations, the Thugs would steal through it in groups of three, silently strangling as many people as they could, using their CUMMERBUNDS, turbans or head scarves. The bodies were either buried or thrown into wells, leaving the Thugs to make off with the spoils. In the days when India was made up of a series of self-governing provinces, some travelling caravans were never reported missing and the crimes could go undetected.

The earliest written record of the Thugs as an identifiable group is in *Tarikh-i-Firuz Shahi* (*Firuz Shah's History*), written by Muslim historian Ziauddin Barani in 1357. According to Barani:

In the region of that sultan [a predecessor of Firuz Shah], around 1290, some thugs were captured in Delhi and one of them was the means of about one thousand being captured. But not one of these did the sultan have killed. Instead he gave orders for them to be put into boats and taken into the lower country, to the region of Lakhnauti where they were to be set free. The thugs would thus have to dwell in Lakhnauti and not cause any trouble in Delhi anymore.

With this opportunity to put an end to the Thugs wasted, the bandits flourished all over the Indian subcontinent for the next 600 years, until the British colonialists were able to suppress them in the 1830s. The British had, after all, been combating piracy on the high seas for over 200 years and were well equipped to deal with its land-based equivalent. When British soldier and administrator William Henry Sleeman captured a leading Thug, one Syeed Amir Ali, he persuaded the bandit to take him to the mass grave of hundreds of caravaners, to explain the circumstances of their deaths and to name those responsible. This tactic provided the British with invaluable leads, and they extended this policy of honesty in return for protection to all Thugs captured thereafter. The thousands who refused were executed. It was Syeed Amir Ali's life story that inspired Philip Meadows Taylor's novel *The Confessions of a Thug* (1839), which was a favourite book of Queen Victoria's.

We've all been made a **scapegoat** at some point in our lives – that is, been blamed for somebody else's mistakes. But what has taking responsibility for something got to do with escaping goats?

The expression dates back to an ancient Hebrew ritual for the Day of Atonement, as set out by none other than Moses himself. The old man decreed that two goats should be taken to the altar of the Tabernacle, where the high priest would draw lots, designating one goat for God and one for Azazel, thought by many to represent the devil. The goat selected as the Lord's would be sacrificed, and the high priest would then, by a process of confession, transfer all of his and his people's sins on to the second goat. The lucky creature would then be allowed to escape into the wilderness, becoming the 'escaped goat' in the process and taking all the sins with it. If only it were that easy these days.

Skulduggery, a truly wonderful English word, is used to describe unscrupulous deeds, usually conducted in secret, conjuring up images of the murky world of body-snatching, which was rife during the eighteenth century. There is no written record of the expression until 1867, however, when it was noted during a political exchange: 'From Minnesota has been imported the mysterious term "scull-duggery," used to signify political trickery.' A few years later, in 1873, another such exchange was recorded for the Official Report of the Debates of the Third Constitutional Convention of Ohio, which suggests that the word had yet to become well known:

> Mr West: 'It is urged upon the assumption that there are some gentlemen here characterized as smouzling.'
> Mr Hadley: 'And what is that?'
> Mr West: 'Skulduggery.'
> Mr Hadley: 'Well, what does that mean?'
> Mr West: 'I don't know what that means, but that is what I heard talked about here.'

But for the actual origin of 'skulduggery', we need to hop back across the Atlantic, to Scotland. During the Jacobite Rebellions of 1715 and 1745, vast numbers of Scottish emigrants sailed to America as English rule tightened its grip north of the border. The Highland Clearances led to further migration, and by 1776 a quarter of a million Scots had found sanctuary on the other side of the water. While many of them would have been villains, criminals, peasants and paupers, they would all have known the Old Scottish term for indecency or ADULTERY, 'sculduddery', which is most likely the root of the word we still use today to describe underhand behaviour.

A **charlatan** is someone who claims to possess certain skills or knowledge but who is instead an impostor or con artist. The term was first applied in the seventeenth century to quack doctors who peddled dubious remedies claiming they could bring about miracle cures. But the practice was not confined to the seventeenth century: one of the most infamous charlatans was a white man who dressed up as 'Sequoia', a Native American, and toured late nineteenth-century England with his band of Redskins, supplying Indian oil that supposedly could cure all manner of ailments. Naturally he was long gone by the time anybody realised they had been taken for a very elaborate ride.

A century earlier, Dr Samuel Johnson, of dictionary fame, claimed he had met the original charlatan, a man called 'Latan' who toured Paris in a fine carriage wearing either a brass helmet or a distinctive feathered hat and distributing potions and cures. When people saw him approaching with his collection of remedies, they would supposedly cry, 'Voilà le char de Latan' – *char* in this case meaning 'carriage'. It's a good story but unlikely to be true. According to the *Oxford English Dictionary*, the word actually comes from the Italian *ciarlatano*, 'BABBLING or chattering', while the etymologist Hugh Rawson goes a step further and suggests *ciarlatano* itself evolved from *cerretano*, an inhabitant of the central Italian village of Cerreto di Spoleto, which in the Middle Ages was the epicentre of the trade in falsified Papal pardons.

When something is **phoney**, meaning 'fake', it is not the genuine article. It comes from the Gaelic *fáinne* (pronounced 'fawnya'), meaning 'circle' or 'ring'. In the eighteenth century, there were widespread doubts as to the authenticity of some imported Irish gold, and by the early nineteenth century gold rings from the Emerald Isle were known as *fawney*, a slang word for 'fake'. During the 1920s, imitation gold rings passed on by American confidence tricksters were also referred to as 'fawney', although the American accent led to further corruption of the word, which had become 'phoney' by the time it arrived on these shores.

A **rookie** is an inexperienced person, usually in his or her first year of a sporting career or other occupation. There have been some far-fetched suggestions for its origins, including the idea that it evolved from the least effective piece on a chessboard, a rook.

A more convincing explanation is that it relates to the crow-like bird known as a rook, which has historically been the scourge of farmers and led to the use of scarecrows to deter such birds from stealing their crops. By the end of the sixteenth century, 'to rook' a person meant to rob, cheat or swindle them (see also DIDDLED), hence people who were easy targets became known as 'rooks', from which it's an easy step to 'rook' or 'rookie' as a term for someone lacking inexperience. The most likely origin of the word is far simpler than that, however: a corruption of the word 'recruit'.

Prior to the invention of toolboxes, all crafts- and tradesmen carried their tools around in a sack. To have one's sack returned – literally 'given the sack' or **sacked** – was to be dismissed, forced to take one's tools elsewhere. Miners who were caught stealing coal or other natural resources such as copper or tin, however, would have their tools confiscated and burned at the pit head in front of the other shift workers, a punishment that became known as 'firing the tools' or just 'being **fired**'. This obviously meant the banished offender would be unable to find other work and repeat his crime elsewhere. That's the story, anyway. It's more likely that 'fired' comes from the expression 'discharged from duty', given the two meanings of the verb 'discharge': to send packing and to fire a gun. Either way, you were out on your ear.

A **patsy** is an innocent person who has been deliberately placed in a position of blame, taking responsibility for another's crimes. It was a popular word during the American gangster era of the 1920s, when a criminal boss would need a patsy to go to jail on his behalf. Perhaps the most famous patsy in history – depending on where you stand on conspiracy theories – is Lee Harvey Oswald, who was himself shot two days after supposedly assassinating John F. Kennedy, arguably because he knew too much.

But the original patsy was Patsy Bolivar, stage persona of the vaudeville entertainer Billy B. Van. Patsy (1878–1950) – claimed by some critics to be the obvious inspiration for Harpo Marx as he appeared in the Marx Brothers films – was a disruptive office boy in shorts, a gingham shirt and a red wig, who was forever being blamed for the comic mishaps of the older characters.

But while Billy B. Van's 'patsy' brought the new word to a wide audience, he wasn't in fact the first Patsy Bolivar. Henry Frederic Reddall's 1899 book *Fact, Fancy and Fable* included a section entitled 'Patsy Bolivar', which told the true story of a group of travelling minstrels who performed a play in Boston in around 1880. One of the characters in the play's country-school setting was a well-behaved little fellow called Patsy Bolivar, who sat quietly in a corner studying his books while a few older boys took turns annoying their schoolmaster. It was a running joke that, whenever the tutor's patience ran out, he would turn around in a rage and demand, 'Who did that?' To which the older boys would chant, 'Patsy, Patsy', and the youngster would be punished. (Oh, the fun they had in those days.) The character clearly caught the public's imagination and, helped along by Billy B. Van's popular act, the word 'patsy' quickly spread.

German migration to America during the nineteenth century (see DUDE) is almost certainly the reason for the word **doppelgänger** – a person who is the (possibly evil) double of another – becoming part of the English language. First used by the German Romantic writer Jean Paul in *Siebenkäs* (1796–7) to describe the alter ego of the novel's hero, the word is formed from a combination of the German words *Doppel*, 'double', and *Gänger*, 'walker' or 'goer'.

To **badger** somebody is to harass or HECTOR them. Back in the good old days, badger-baiting was another of those quaint English pastimes in which dogs would be set upon defenceless creatures in the name of sport (see BULLDOG). In this case, the badger would be trapped, thrown into a barrel that was open at one end, and the dogs would be sent in after it. This was known as 'badgering'. The popularity of badgering was on the wane by the time the Cruelty to Animals Act was passed in 1835, although it was replaced, for a time, by dog-fighting.

In nineteenth-century North America, badgers were considered a nuisance and would be tracked by farmers over a number of days, and then either poisoned or shot. This relentless pursuit was also known as badgering.

Hectoring is a form of bullying or browbeating, usually verbal rather than physical. In *The Iliad*, Homer's account of the Trojan Wars, Hector is the son of the Trojan king Priam and the brother of Paris, whose abduction of Helen of Troy (who was in fact from Sparta) sparked the conflict in the first place. As the noblest and bravest of all of the Trojans, Hector featured prominently on the battlefield, persistently harassing the Greeks over a ten-year period. But when he made the mistake of killing Patroclus, the ally and closest friend of the almost-invincible Greek warrior Achilles, the latter exacted his revenge by slaying Hector and having him dragged in triumph around the walls of Troy.

By the seventeenth century, however, when the restoration of the monarchy led to the restoration of the theatrical arts following their suppression under Cromwell, Hector's role in history had somehow become distorted and the great Trojan warrior was portrayed on stage as a blustering bully. By the later years of that century, gangs of rowdy RUFFIANS were known as 'Hectors' and it wasn't long before 'hectoring' became the byword for any form of intimidation and bullying.

LAW AND ORDER

Karma, as far as the Hindu faith and Buddhism are concerned, is the concept that a person's own actions will bring comparable results, good or bad, whether in this life or the next. We will be rewarded or punished according to how well we behave: good things happen to good people and bad things happen to bad. First recorded as part of the English language in around 1820, the word evolved from the Sanskrit word *karman*, which means 'action' or 'deed'.

You may recall from your school days that, in French, *avocat* means both AVOCADO and 'lawyer', but this is deceptive: the English noun **advocate** has little to do with fruit, pear-shaped or otherwise. It comes instead, as many of our legal terms do, from the Latin, from the word *advocatus*, meaning 'legal witness'. There is, however, a tenuous connection. To 'swear on your testicles' is an old phrase that supposedly refers to the custom, in the courtrooms of ancient Rome, for a man to place his right hand on that part of his anatomy while swearing to the truth of a statement. It's a great idea but one which has probably arisen as a result of the word *testis*, in Latin, meaning both 'testicle' and 'witness'. *Testis* itself comes from an Indo-European word for the number three and was applied by the Romans to a third party, hence 'witness', who could provide objective evidence in a court case. Therefore when a Roman gentleman in court was 'swearing on his testicles', he was actually swearing on the truth of his evidence as a witness, although I bet that hasn't stopped students of Roman law sniggering over the double-entendre.

Sheriff is a word that evokes images of the American Wild West, with the likes of Pat Garrett jumping on to his horse to hunt down Billy the Kid. But the word 'sheriff' can be traced back by quite a few centuries, dating to that innocent time when England was made up of dozens of self-governing shires, similar to modern-day counties, only a lot smaller. The Old English spelling of the word was *scir*, to rhyme with 'dire', and it translated as 'division of land'.

It was William the Conqueror (see BASTARD) who turned the sprawling Anglo-Saxon shire network into something more efficient and controllable, having determined via the Domesday Book, recording the survey conducted throughout England and parts of Wales, what and who was in his new kingdom. He also standardised the titles of administrative officials, known as 'reeves': there was the high-reeve, the port-reeve in towns by the coast or a river, the town-reeve and, of course, the shire-reeve – the origin of the word now used to indicate the good GUY in cowboy films and the arch baddie in those starring Robin Hood.

To this day, the word 'sheriff' is still used in England in reference to a legal official with ceremonial duties, in Scotland for a judge and in America for a variety of positions depending upon which state you are in, but always relating to the legal profession or the police.

In grand medieval households, the responsibility for law and order traditionally fell to a **constable**. The word comes from the Latin *comes stabuli*, 'count of the stables'. Guarding the horses of any emperor or military leader was an important job in Roman times, but constables had taken on a broader portfolio by the later Middle Ages, guarding the land for whatever lord or landowner employed them.

Over the centuries, their numbers and duties steadily increased, prompting Home Secretary (later Prime Minister) Sir Robert Peel to organise these law-enforcers into a police force, under the Metropolitan Police Act of 1829. It was thanks to him that the police earned their first two NICKNAMES, **bobbies** and **peelers**.

Have you ever wondered why we call those unreconstructed Neanderthals who work in the private security industry, generally loitering menacingly in the doorways of places you would never want to go into, **bouncers**? During the latter part of the nineteenth century, American saloon owners and those who ran houses of ill-repute began employing SHERIFFS and other security men to prevent rowdy and drunken customers from harassing the bar girls. In modern times, of course, customers are more likely to need protection from the bouncers themselves.

The word was popularised by the prolific author Horatio Alger, Jr., whose novel *The Young Outlaw; or, Adrift in the Streets* (1875) included a chapter entitled 'Bounced', in which Sam, the penniless young hero, is thrown out of a restaurant when it is discovered he does not have enough money to pay for his meal. The following passage inspired the name we now give to the hundreds of thousands of monosyllabic, neckless bullies who have been patrolling our pavements ever since.

'Here, Peter, you waited on this young man didn't you?'

'Yes, sir.'

'He hasn't paid for his breakfast, and pretends he hasn't got any money. *Bounce him!*'

If Sam was ignorant of the meaning of 'bounce,' he was enlightened. The waiter seized him by the collar, before he knew what was going to happen, pushed him to the door, and then, lifting his foot with a well-directed kick, landed him across the sidewalk into the street.

This proceeding was followed by derisive laughter from the other waiters who had gathered near the door . . . Sam staggered from the force of the bouncing, and felt disgraced and humiliated to think the waiter who had been so respectful and attentive should have inflicted upon him such an indignity, which he had no power to resent.

It seems to me that young Alger had not only given the profession a name, but also written the job description.

A **bigwig** is somebody in authority, one of society's movers and shakers. The word comes from seventeenth-century England, when it was fashionable for gentlemen to wear wigs, a tradition that lasts to this day among judges and members of the House of Lords. The seventeenth-century craze for wig wearing was not only an indication of style, however, but also an indication of status: the more elaborate and expensive the wig, the more important the wig wearer. The aristocracy, bishops and High Court judges were all accorded full-length wigs to represent their position at the top of society, as a result of which they became known as 'bigwigs'. The tradition is fading these days, however, as many High Court judges opt not to wear their big wigs, believing this practice makes the judiciary look outdated and out of touch. And they think that is the only thing!

The kind of young GYPSIES we are sadly becoming used to seeing on TV might well find themselves ending up in **borstal**, a corrective training centre for young offenders. The word is often thought to be a corruption of 'board-school', in the sense that naughty schoolboys had to board there, but its origin is much simpler than that: the first such establishment was built in 1902 in the village of Borstal in Kent. By the turn of the twentieth century, the quaint old Victorian custom of throwing children into adult prisons had been banned and young offenders were sent to Borstal instead. The apparent success of this system led to many more 'borstals' cropping up across the country. Coincidentally, 'Borstal', as in the name of the village, comes from the Old English *borg*, meaning 'fortress', and *steall*, which in turn translates as 'place'.

A **muckraker** is known for his or her ability to discover and reveal a scandal. Usually muckrakers are journalists, pamphlet writers or, increasingly these days, bloggers, although the art of **muckraking** is also alive and well in the world of office politics.

The word has been in regular use since, specifically, 14 April 1906, when President Theodore Roosevelt delivered a famous speech during which he invited his audience to 'recall the description of the Man with the Muck Rake, the man who could look no way but downward, with the muck rake in his hand'. During the same speech Roosevelt also warned that 'The men with the muck rakes are often indispensable to the wellbeing of society; but only if they know when to stop raking the muck.'

The president was referring to the new breed of fearless, investigative journalists that had emerged in America during the later decades of the nineteenth century, and who were determined to reveal injustice and corruption at the heart of what was supposed to be the land of freedom and opportunity. Magazines such as *Collier's Weekly*, established in 1888, were considered to be pioneers of investigative journalism; after attempts by major corporations to sue the popular magazine failed, other periodicals such as *McClure's* pitched in, feeding the growing market of the aspiring middle classes with revelations about their oppressive overlords.

A perfect example of how far the muckrakers were prepared to go in order to reveal injustice came in 1872, when journalist Julius Chambers had himself committed to the Bloomingdale Insane Asylum with the intention of obtaining information about the alleged abuse of inmates. After a ten-day stint inside, his magazine editor arranged for his release and the resulting series of articles, published in the *Tribune*, led to the release of a dozen inmates who were not actually insane, a complete overhaul of that particular asylum, and ultimately a change in the government's attitude towards 'lunacy'. With that, Chambers had spearheaded the kind of 'muckraking' – or, as some call it, 'drain sniffing' – that is such an integral part of investigative journalism to this day. Good work, Julius.

Although this was how the word was popularised across the English-speaking world, 'muckraking' was by no means a new concept. When he made his 1906 speech, Roosevelt was in fact quoting John Bunyan's religious narrative *Pilgrim's Progress* (1678), which features an allegorical character whose 'muck-rake doth show his carnal mind . . . to show that Heaven is but as a fable to some, and that things here are counted the only things substantial'.

When NGOs – non-governmental organisations – were dreamt up in the mid-twentieth century, the idea was that they would act as regulators for various industries. They would essentially perform government functions without outside pressure or influence from government or business leaders. It all seemed like a great idea until the 1980s, when it was realised that there were far too many NGOs whose impartiality was questionable. This led to the derogatory term 'quasi-autonomous non-governmental organisation', or **quango**. In 2007, the British pressure group TaxPayers' Alliance revealed that the number of publicly funded quangos was in excess of 1,000, at a cost of around £64 billion. Which may well have signalled the end of the quangos, since their numbers are beginning to be reduced. Call me cynical but I can only imagine they'll eventually be replaced by something similar, so that former Members of Parliament and ageing Lords have a highly paid job to get up for in the morning.

As well as being the name of an Olympic sport for very bendy people, the **high jump** – as in the expression **for the high jump** – is used to refer to an imminent punishment or reprimand. This figurative use of the word is a reference to death by hanging, which was the most common form of capital punishment in Britain until the abolition of the death penalty under the strangely named Murder Act of 1965.

Hanging traditionally involved the condemned approaching the gallows on a horse, cart or ladder that was then moved away, leaving him dangling and strangling. Over the final century of capital punishment, however, the whole process of hanging was made much more humane, first thanks to the 'standard drop' method recommended by Irish doctor Samuel Haughton, and subsequently by the 'variable drop' (or 'measured drop') introduced by executioner William Marwood in the 1870s. Both methods were designed to ensure the neck was broken as soon as the prisoner dropped from the gallows, although the latter improved on the former by tailoring the length of the drop according to a prisoner's weight, so as to avoid decapitation.

In the Royal Navy one of the favoured methods of execution was to throw a rope over the yardarm and launch

141

a man into the air in front of his crewmates. You might think that watching your shipmate swinging overhead with his legs kicking about would be an effective deterrent, but there are many recorded hangings in this manner, which was known in the fleet as the 'high jump'.

Lynching is associated with Lynch's Mob, the original lynch mob. American lynch mobs were most prominent in the Southern states (see DIXIELAND) during the second half of the nineteenth century; in ten states alone, authorities recorded 2,805 deaths at the hands of the mobs between 1882 and 1930. Of the victims 2,500 were black, hanged without trial for their perceived crimes.

The original Lynch is thought to be Captain William Lynch (1742–1820) of Pittsylvania County, Virginia, who in 1780 signed a formal agreement with his neighbours to deal with local criminals without troubling the legal authorities. He formed a group of men and declared that if the trouble-makers 'will not desist from their evil practices, we shall inflict such corporeal punishment on him or them, as to us shall seem adequate to the crime committed or the damage sustained'. The kind of vigilante justice meted out by Lynch's Mob became known as 'Lynch's Law', and was at that time restricted to horsewhippings and beatings rather than executions. An October 1835 edition of the *New England Magazine* ran the headline 'The Inconveniences of Being Lynched', while a piece from the *New York Daily Express* in

1843 tells of a person who was 'lately taken from his house at night by some of his neighbours and severely lynched [thrashed]'. White supremacists subsequently adopted the comparatively harmless word for their own campaign of terror, and that's where it has stayed ever since.

MILITARY AND NAUTICAL

Shrapnel is a fascinating term that sounds as though it must have been around for ever, one of those words in English clearly reflecting its Scandinavian roots. Sadly, this impression is completely wrong, however, for the word itself is far more recent in origin.

It has evolved in meaning too. The modern dictionary definition of 'shrapnel' is 'fragments of an exploding bomb', whereas originally, during the First World War, it meant the whole explosive device, not just parts of it. 'Shrapnel-shells' were designed as anti-personnel artillery, packed with bullets that would discharge close to the target with the obvious intention of killing or maiming as many of the enemy as possible. Shrapnel-shells were far more effective for the purpose than a conventional bomb, but they became obsolete at the end of the war when they were replaced with high-explosive shells, which did much the same job but whose deadly fragments were still known as 'shrapnel'.

The original First World War weapon was named after Major General Henry Shrapnel (1761–1842), a British army officer and inventor who served in the Royal Artillery during the Napoleonic Wars (1803–15). He devised a hollow cannonball filled with grapeshot, which was attached to a rocket and designed to burst in mid-air, creating multiple casualties. Shrapnel's idea was not to kill enemy soldiers but to maim them, since a dead man needs no immediate attention whereas a wounded one requires the attention of at least two others, if only to remove him from the battlefield. Such was the success of his invention that Henry Shrapnel was awarded over £1,000 in 1814, a considerable sum of money in those days, and in 1827 was promoted to the post of Colonel Commandant of the Royal Artillery.

The first verse of the American national anthem proudly describes the Americans resisting an onslaught of shrapnel by the British army during the pivotal Battle of Baltimore in 1812: 'And the rockets' red glare, the bombs bursting in air, / Gave proof through the night that our flag was still there.'

Going at something **gung ho** used to mean approaching a task in an enthusiastic and committed way. It also tended to mean you were American. These days, in most of the English-speaking world, it is more often associated with carelessness and a lack of concern for consequences. Brigadier-General Evans Fordyce Carlson (1896–1947) found fame during the Second World War as the leader of Carlson's Raiders, a US Marine Corp unit that attacked Makin Island, deep behind the Japanese lines, in 1942. This offensive itself could certainly have been described as gung-ho, but it was not until the following year that Carlson brought the word to prominence.

During an interview in 1943, he explained how he had learned the expression 'gung ho' from his New Zealand friend the communist writer Rewi Alley, who had helped found the Chinese Industrial Cooperatives in 1938 in support of the War of Resistance against Japan. The slogan of that movement was Gung Ho (*gonghe* in Chinese), meaning 'to work together in harmony' – an ethos Carlson was trying to promote throughout the rank and file by holding a series of Gung Ho meetings. 'I was trying to find a way of building up the same sort of working spirit I had seen in China,' he said, 'where all the soldiers dedicated themselves to one idea and worked together to put that idea across. I told the boys time and time again, and that the motto of the Chinese Cooperatives is Gung Ho. It means work together, work in harmony.'

Despite Carlson's noble intentions, however, the word's association with bravery, recklessness and spirit was cemented that same year, with the release of a rousing movie about Carlson's Raiders starring Randolph Scott, and simply entitled *Gung Ho!*

A bat horse (short for 'battling horse') was a pack horse used by officers of the British army during the First World War to carry their personal belongings; the junior soldier charged with taking responsibility for these possessions and filling the role of general servant consequently became known as the **batman**. And that is why, in some military circles and upper echelons of British society, the master's personal valet is still called the 'batman' – and not because he dresses up in tights and fights crime in Gotham City. During the Second World War, Lieutenant-Colonel David Niven and Private Peter Ustinov were working on a film together as actor and writer, respectively. The difference in their ranks apparently made it so unseemly for them to be seen socially together that Niven had to appoint Ustinov his batman, probably the second most famous Batman after the celluloid one.

When something is blown to **smithereens** it has been shattered into thousands of small pieces. This expression is of Gaelic origin and means 'small or tiny fragments'. The Gaelic spelling of the word is *smidirín*, which leads us to a modern Irish expression for a severe hangover. To be **in schmids** (in pieces) is an evocative phrase used to express a sorry state of affairs the morning after – which, I understand, is most mornings in Ireland.

When two or more people are at **loggerheads** they are generally engaged in a confrontation of some sort. It is an expression that originated in the late sixteenth century, when it was brought to prominence by William Shakespeare. At this time, a 'logger' was the word for a heavy wooden block fastened to the legs of a grazing horse to give it enough leeway to move around slowly but not enough to run away or jump over fences. These wooden blocks would quite often get tangled together, causing the horses to which they were attached to jostle and fight in agitation. Shakespeare used the phrase in *The Taming of the Shrew* (1592), in which Petruchio castigates his incompetent attendants as 'logger-headed grooms'.

An alternative theory relates to nautical warfare in the ancient world. In this context, a loggerhead was a weapon: a long pole with a cup fixed to the end, which was used to project hot tar at enemy ships in order to set fire to them. If both sides happened to be using the same weapon, they were, of course, 'at loggerheads'.

As with GOLLIWOG, it can be difficult to peel away the offensive modern meaning of a word from its benign historical one. Take the **swastika**, for instance. In the 1920s, the German Nazi Party adopted the distinctive hooked cross, or *Hakenkreuz*, that was later to become such a potent symbol of hate, repression and racism; to display one anywhere, under any circumstances, nowadays would be considered unbelievably offensive.

Which is a shame, in a way, because for thousands of years

before Hitler and his jackbooted goons marched all over the pages of history, the identical-looking *svastika*, which in Sanskrit means 'auspicious' or 'lucky', has been a religious symbol and sign of good fortune. Indeed, the earliest examples of the swastika can be traced as far back as the Indus Valley civilisation of the second and third millennia BC.

Although the swastika is still widely used today in Indian religions such as Jainism, Hinduism and Buddhism – it is one of the 108 symbols of the Hindu god Vishnu, representing the life-giving rays of the sun – the idea of a young Buddhist proudly sporting a swastika T-shirt while walking down Oxford Street doesn't really bear thinking about.

The word **jingo** – which later spawned **jingoism** – emerged around the mid-seventeenth century in the phrase 'by jingo', used as a euphemism for 'by Jesus'. In the form 'Hey jingo', it was uttered by conjurers and street magicians in London as part of their act, to accompany the magical appearance of an object. It was in a similar vein to 'Hey presto', to mean 'as if by magic', *presto* being the Italian for 'quick' or 'speed', reflecting how many of London's street magicians at the time would have been immigrants from what is now known as Italy.

At the end of that century, Pierre Antoine Motteux's acclaimed translation of the works of French satirist François Rabelais used 'by jingo' as the English version of *par-Dieu*, which literally means 'by God'. But two centuries later, this relatively innocent little word had evolved into a highly derogatory one, to describe aggressive so-called patriotism: 'jingoism'.

During the 1800s, Britain was almost continuously at war. If it wasn't the French (Napoleonic Wars: 1803–15) or the Russians (Crimean War: 1853–6), it was the Indians (Indian Rebellion: 1857) or the South Africans (Boer Wars: 1880–1902); at virtually no point in the nineteenth century was Britain at complete peace. As a result, patriotism and propaganda were of vital importance to the morale of the nation. Ironically, however, it was a war the British managed *not* to get involved in that led to 'jingoism' becoming an established part of the English language.

During the Russo-Turkish War of 1877–8, when the Russians threatened to occupy the port of Constantinople (now Istanbul), anti-Russian feeling ran high across Britain and Prime Minister Benjamin Disraeli ordered the Mediterranean fleet to help defend the Turkish capital. The subsequent stand-off between the Russians and the British was a tense one, but the British, as usual, were fully prepared for war. It was against this backdrop that a songwriter called G. W. Hunt wrote a rousing and popular music-hall anthem that included the lines:

We don't want to fight, but by Jingo if we do,
We've got the ships, we've got the men, and we've
    got the money too.

> We've fought the Bear before, and while we are
>   Britons true,
> The Russians shall not have Constantinople too.

And that is how 'jingoism' – 'warlike patriotism' – evolved from the street magicians of old London town.

D-Day must be one of the most famous words in military history. Although the 'D' is often thought to be for 'Deliverance', it in fact stands, in military parlance, for 'day' – in the same way as the 'H' in 'H-Hour' stands for 'hour'. It is simply a way of counting down to an offensive without giving away the actual time or date, the day before D-Day being D-1, and so on. The most famous D-Day of them all, of course, was 6 June 1944, when Britain and her allies launched an offensive across the English Channel at the start of the campaign to free France from occupation by Nazi Germany.

But this wasn't the first D-Day in military history: there were also a number of them during the First World War. Field orders dated 7 September 1918, for instance, read: 'The First Army will attack at H-Hour on D-Day.' Later in the twentieth century, 'D-Day' was used by some to signify 15 February 1971, the day the decimal currency was introduced to Britain, but for me and millions of others there is only ever going to be one D-Day, and that's *the* D-Day of 1944.

A **turncoat** is someone who switches allegiance during a dispute or battle, generally without hesitation or remorse. One fairly simplistic theory about its origin is that the word refers to retreating soldiers who turned their topcoats around and wore them back to front in the hope nobody would realise they were running away rather than facing the enemy. But this is ridiculous. Unless the deserters in question also managed to shave the backs of their heads and paint on a face and moustache, this ruse couldn't have occurred frequently enough for the word for it to have passed into common parlance.

Instead, there is a slightly more plausible story behind the expression. It concerns the Hundred Years' War of the fourteenth and fifteenth centuries, during which the Duke of Saxony – whose land occupied an area long fought over by the French and the English – cleverly took to wearing a coat that was blue on one side and white on the reverse. When the French army was on his land, he wore the white side to match their colour, and when the English army gained ground he turned it inside out and wore it as a blue coat, affecting loyalty to them instead.

Dog-tired is an expression of absolute exhaustion or fatigue. It comes from the Royal Navy's peacetime watch system, which was first developed in the seventeenth century and subsequently adopted by so many other navies that there has never been any reason to modify it.

At sea, it is vital for a ship to be manned twenty-four hours a day, and there are three crucial areas that must never be left unattended: the bridge, the ship's control centre and the main communications office. To ensure sufficient manpower at all times, the crew's working day is split into four-hour shifts, with the exception of the last watch, or 'dog watch', which is made up of two two-hour shifts.

Time	Name
2000–0000	First watch
0000–0400	Middle watch
0400–0800	Morning watch
0800–1200	Forenoon watch
1200–1600	Afternoon watch
1600–1800	First dog watch
1800–2000	Last dog watch

The 'dog watch' has always been split into two so that all the sailors have a chance to eat their evening meal. Its name, from which 'dog-tired' developed, is thought to be a corruption of 'dodge watch', a NICKNAME given to it by early mariners who considered the half-watch a cop-out. Traditionally – harking back to the days when the watches didn't have watches – bells have marked each half-hour of a watch, with eight bells indicating knocking-off time. Interestingly, the number of bells sounded at the end of a dog watch is not 1-2-3-4-5-6-7-8 but rather 1-2-3-4-1-2-3-8, a tradition that goes back to 1797, when a group of mutineers planned to seize control of a ship at 'five bells in the dog watches', after which officers decreed that only one bell should be struck at 6.30 p.m., instead of five.

To commit **hara-kiri** is to take one's own life, although it can be used in a more figurative sense to describe someone who has recklessly, and often quite publicly, scuppered their own political or business career.

In Japan, the act of hara-kiri traditionally involved ritually disembowelling oneself after being disgraced or dishonoured. A military defeat may bring such a shame, as might being caught with another person's wife, or with your hand in his cash sack. The act of hara-kiri would be performed with great ceremony and often in front of an audience, and indeed it was an obligatory punishment for certain kinds of 'disgrace' until 1873.

The term has often been translated into English as the 'happy dispatch', although it is in fact made up of *hara*, a slang word for 'belly', and *kiri*, 'to cut'. Ironically, the Japanese tend to use a different word for hara-kiri, *seppuku*, which is a corruption of *setsu*, meaning 'to cut', and *fuku*, 'abdomen'.

To go **berserk** is to be in an uncontrollably wild and violent state. There is a tale in Norse mythology about a certain warrior who dressed only in a bearskin coat and would work himself into a frenzy before going into battle. The story goes that he would throw down his weapons and fight bare-handed. This warrior was universally feared – as were his twelve sons, each of whom had a fearsome reputation of his own. Their battle dress earned them a NICKNAME: 'berserkers', a combination of the words *bern*, 'bear', and *serkr*, 'coat'. Many Scandinavian warriors emulated their formidable heroes, and the word crossed the North Sea to England during the ninth-century Viking invasion.

To ride **roughshod** over someone is to treat them harshly and without consideration for their feelings. Horses that are roughshod have the nails protruding from their shoes, something that used to be done deliberately in order to provide extra grip in wet or icy conditions. But to be trampled on or kicked by a roughshod horse is a little uncomfortable, to say the least. In the eighteenth century, it was common for cavalry soldiers from many countries to ensure their horses were roughshod or had other sharp objects attached to their hoofs, the idea being that the horses would cut and damage enemy mounts with their sharp shoes. The practice ultimately resulted in horses doing more damage to themselves than to others, and it was quickly phased out.

LANGUAGE, LITERATURE AND THE PERFORMING ARTS

The French-born British writer and cartoonist George du Maurier (1834–96) has had a number of little-known but lasting effects on the English language – and that is even before we consider that his grandsons were the inspiration for J. M. Barrie's *Peter Pan* and that his granddaughter was the novelist Daphne du Maurier.

As a cartoonist, du Maurier worked for *Punch* magazine, turning his satirical observations of Victorian society into an art form. One of his most famous cartoons, in which a polite curate assures his host that parts of a rotten egg he has been served 'are excellent', gave rise to the expression **curate's egg**, which is still used to describe something that is partly good and partly awful. In 1884, du Maurier also coined the phrase **bedside manner**, as a caption to a cartoon that satirised medical practices of the era.

As his eyesight deteriorated, du Maurier retired to Hampstead in north London, where he wrote three novels, two of which were published during his lifetime. The second, a bestseller called *Trilby* (1894), is the story of a struggling young artist's model called Trilby O'Ferrall, who falls under the spell of an evil music agent called **Svengali**; he transforms her into an international sensation, but only so long as she remains under his hypnotic spell. In one of the illustrations, du Maurier drew a soft felt hat with a narrow brim and indented crown, which was made and worn for the stage production of the book, since when the **trilby** hat has been so named.

A **potboiler** is a piece of 'art' – usually a painting or a book – that cynically panders to popular taste. The term is often misused in the case of soap operas to suggest that the drama is so good that the 'pot is kept boiling' for another week. But its true meaning is certainly derisory rather than complimentary. Real potboilers are intended to ensure a steady flow of income for an artist's family, keeping food bubbling in the kitchen pot, until a more imaginative commission comes along.

I have often wondered why we call a level of a building a **storey** when it has nothing to do with the telling of tales, so I was interested to stumble across an explanation that links the two.

'Story', of course, means a 'narrative of fictitious events', and it is derived from the ancient Greek *historia*, 'account of events'. *Historia* is also the root of our 'history', meaning 'factual account', from which we can infer that the difference between 'history' and 'story' is the difference between fact and fiction. Following this so far? Now for the tricky bit.

Back in the fourteenth century, before the Caxton printing press changed everything, the word 'story' was used in architecture in the sense that stained-glass windows and stone carvings or sculptures on the outsides of buildings carried stories in their theme. The more rows of pictures on a building, the more stories it was able to tell. This kind of architectural story gradually developed into the more mundane 'storey' of modern times: an entire level of a building. I'm glad I found that out, as I can now view my local multi-storey car park with a whole new respect.

We all love a good **limerick**, don't we? And the cheekier the better, like this one making fun of one of the great figures of classical times:

> Archimedes, the famous truth-seeker,
> Leapt out of the bath, cried 'Eureka!'
> Then ran half a mile
> Wearing only a smile
> And became the first ever streaker.

The Victorian poet and author Edward Lear (1812–88) popularised the limerick, notably in his *Book of Nonsense* (1846), which remains in print to this day. The earliest example of limerick-style poetry in print, however, is an anonymous ballad named 'Tom a BEDLAM', thought to have been published in around 1600. It begins:

> From the hag and hungry goblin
> That into rags would rend ye,
> The spirit that stands
> By the naked man
> In the book of moons defend ye.

But there has been some debate as to how the word 'limerick' became associated with cheeky five-line poems. Given that Edward Lear never actually used the word himself, there is speculation that it emerged after his death as a mispronunciation of 'Learic'. A more plausible theory is that the word has something to do with the city or county of the same name in Ireland, although the exact connection is unclear.

One suggestion is that it was inspired by a group of eighteenth-century Gaelic poets who met regularly at a pub in Croom, in the Maigue Valley of County Limerick. Two members of the group – which was known as the *Fili na Maighe*, 'poets of the Maigue'– were Aindrias MacCraith and Sean O'Tuama, who certainly wrote popular songs in the style of what is now known as a limerick, although the word did not officially enter the English language in connection with poetry until over a century later, when it appeared in the *New English Dictionary* of 1898. It is safe to assume the term would have been in use during at least the latter part of Edward Lear's career, but the cynic in me wonders whether the Maigue Poets were a convenient discovery by later historians looking for a satisfactory origin of the word.

There was, however, a popular music-hall refrain in the late nineteenth century that not only used the limerick form but also included a reference to Limerick the place. The audience would participate in a five-line rhyme that would be completed with a cry of 'Won't you come up to Limerick?', which is almost certainly how the city finally became associated with the form of poetry that had already become famous thanks to Edward Lear.

All writers and editors know that to **bowdlerise** a manuscript is to censor passages in it, and no author is ever very happy about that, believe me. But only one editor has ever had the distinction of being so slash-happy with an author's work as to have coined a word – fortunately for him, the author in question had died a couple of centuries earlier.

Thomas Bowdler (1754–1825) trained as a medical student in the late eighteenth century, but upon graduating he found that his own illness and persistent injury, rather ironically, prevented him from practising. After a period of campaigning for prison reform, Bowdler decided to travel to Europe, where he wrote books and pamphlets warning British travellers about the unhygienic conditions of the drinking water in France, and then retired to the Isle of Wight to become an editor.

In 1818, Bowdler proudly published his ten-volume edition of the works of William Shakespeare, declaring: 'Nothing is added to the original text; but those words are omitted which cannot, with any propriety, be read aloud in a family.' In other words, he was censoring it for the preservation of family morals. Expanding on his reasons for this, Bowdler wrote: 'Many words and expressions occur which are of such an indecent nature as to render it highly desirable that they should be erased.'

Publication of this edition was met with immediate complaints from critics and scholars that 'no play of Shakespeare's [had] escaped Bowdler's broad eraser', but the censored version appeared to be exactly what the public wanted; it was reissued eleven times, four of them in Bowdler's lifetime. Flushed with such success, Bowdler turned his attention to Edward Gibbon's seminal *History of the Decline and Fall of the Roman Empire* (1776–89), promising the 'careful omission of all passages of an irreligious or immoral tendency'. Once again, Bowdler's purity crusade attracted a mixture of criticism, controversy and, from some quarters, acclaim. It is generally believed that his sister Harriet was responsible for most of the actual work, but since women of the age were not supposed to publicly demonstrate that they understood anything of a racy or irreligious nature, she could not be given credit for her contribution. After his death, Bowdler's nephew continued the family tradition of sanitising literature, with the result that 'bowdlerise' and **bowdlerism** had become common terms by the 1830s.

A **spoonerism** is an often inadvertent mixing-up of letters or even whole words in a sentence. Technically a form of metathesis – which means the same although 'spoonerism' is a much better word – it can result in someone communicating completely the wrong message, to hilarious effect. For example, you might reveal that you are 'bearing a welt' instead of 'wearing a belt', and we've all fallen foul of the tongue-twister 'I'm not a Pheasant Plucker'. Meanwhile, it's hard to feel sorry for the politician who supposedly wanted to complain to the press about a 'pack of lies' but ended up ranting about a 'lack of pies'.

Although surely not the first to confuse his words in this way, the Reverend W. A. Spooner (1844–1930), Warden of New College, Oxford, in the late nineteenth and early twentieth centuries, is certainly the most famous. Some of his best verbal mix-ups included 'You have been caught fighting a liar in the quad' and 'We all know what it is to have a half-warmed fish inside us'. Spooner, who hated being famous for his 'spoonerisms', is also supposed to have berated a bewildered scholar for 'hissing my mystery lectures', although my personal favourite is his toast at a formal dinner to the 'queer old dean'.

The BBC has broadcast more than its fair share of

Spooner-related bloopers over the years, including repeated references to the 'British Broadcorping Castration' and Barry Cryer's sly description of a prominent TV personality as a 'shining wit' on Radio Four's *Sorry, I Haven't a Clue*. But by far the most famous example came at 7.59 a.m. on 6 December 2010, when veteran broadcaster James Naughtie promised an interview on Radio Four's *Today* programme with the much-maligned Culture Secretary Jeremy Hunt, a name he unfortunately managed to turn into a spoonerism. What exactly is a 'Hulture Secretary' anyway, Jim?

Although similar to a SPOONERISM, a **malapropism** is generally more easily understood and glossed over. It is when a word is substituted for a similar-sounding word with a totally different meaning.

Dear old George W. Bush – who, incredibly, was *not* the subject of a piece I once wrote entitled 'The President's Brain is Missing' – provided journalists with a wealth of malapropisms throughout his tenure at the White House. Some of my favourites include: 'The law I will sign today directs new funds to the task of collecting intelligence of weapons of mass production'; 'They misunderestimated me'; 'It will take time to restore chaos and order'; and 'We cannot let terrorists and rogue nations hold this nation hostile'.

And George Dubya is not alone. Boxer Frank Bruno once threatened (or perhaps confused) Mike Tyson by declaring, 'When I have finished with him he will have channel vision', while TV presenter Cilla Black once asked somebody if they planned to 'abseil across the English Channel'. In 1985, *The Times* reported that a miners' union leader had denounced his company's management as 'totally incontinent', and then there's the lady who famously complained she was not at all 'enamelled with' her new kitchen. (Perhaps all it had needed was a fresh coat of emotion.)

All of these wonderful mistakes can be traced to the Mrs Malaprop, a character in Sheridan's comedy *The Rivals* (1775). Her linguistic errors include 'She's as headstrong as an allegory on the banks of the Nile' and 'Promise to forget this fellow – to illiterate him, I say, quite from your memory'. In naming his character, Sheridan borrowed from the French *mal à propos*, 'not the purpose' or 'not appropriate'.

Before the appearance of Mrs Malaprop, malapropisms were called **dogberryisms**, after the equally inarticulate character Dogberry in Shakespeare's *Much Ado about Nothing* (1598). Dogberry's many gaffes include: 'Our watch, sir, have indeed comprehended two aspicious persons.'

Sports presenter David Coleman became so well known for his mispronunciations and senseless commentary that *Private Eye* magazine coined the term **Colemanballs** to denote any linguistic 'balls-up' in the style of the British television presenter.

Colemanballs are an ill-defined beast but they generally involve an inadvertent double-entendre or nonsensical statement broadcast on TV or radio. Coleman wasn't the only perpetrator of Colemanballs, but that doesn't stop most of them being attributed to him. Famous examples of his include: 'He's just opened his legs wide and showed us his class' (a running commentary on the great Cuban athlete Alberto Juantorena); 'Linford Christie has a habit of pulling it out when it matters most'; 'The Dutch manager told them in the dressing gown at half time'; and the splendid 'For those of you watching in black and white, Everton are in the blue shirts.' Perhaps the most memorable Colemanballs was actually delivered by cricket commentator Brian Johnston: 'The batsman's Holding, the bowler's Willey.'

But Colemanballs aren't restricted to the world of sports commentary: Prime Minister John Major notoriously ballsed up what was meant to be a stern warning when he declared: 'When your back's against the wall, you have to turn round and fight.'

Syntax is the – in case you are wondering, by the way, and as every good writer will tell you – art of using a correctly grammatical arrangement of the sentence's words – or, you know, the art of structuring our sentences properly. Sentences that are improperly formed can result in unintentional and often hilarious ambiguity, such as in these two examples included by Bruce Fraser in his 1973 revision of Sir Ernest Gowers' *The Complete Plain Words* (1948): 'Nothing is less likely to appeal to a young woman than the opinions of old men on the Pill' and 'I have discussed the question of stocking the proposed poultry plant with my colleagues'.

'Syntax', from the Greek *sun*, 'together', and *tassein*, 'arrange', entered the English language towards the end of the sixteenth century. But it wasn't until the early nineteenth century that most people became familiar with the word, thanks to the cartoons engraved by English caricaturist Thomas Rowlandson (1756–1827) to illustrate the comic poem *The Three Tours of Dr Syntax* by William Combe. *The Tour of Dr Syntax in Search of the Picturesque* (1813), *Dr Syntax in Search of Consolation* (1820) and *The Third Tour of Dr Syntax in Search of a Wife* (1821) proved to be so popular with the public that a racehorse was named after the central character, which, at the height of Dr Syntax mania in 1820, went and won the Epsom DERBY, inspiring several pub names in the process.

Babbitt is a word used mainly in America to describe a person who is a self-satisfied, middle-of-the-road conformer to the ideals of business and material success. The original Babbitt was the eponymous antihero of a 1922 novel by Sinclair Lewis (1885–1951), the first American winner of the Nobel Prize for Literature. The novel's success spawned a silent film of the same name.

In the book, George F. Babbitt is a married, 46-year-old real-estate agent with three children and a house in a prosperous area. His constant pursuit of material gain is matched only by his increasing discontent and restless attempts to escape to a more meaningful life, something in which he repeatedly fails. Lewis's comic novel was said to capture the emotions, concerns and vacuity of the white-collar business community of 1920s America. The themes of the book continue to ring true for dissatisfied housewives and their middle-aged, middle-class HUSBANDS, and the derogatory term remains in wide use in America.

To **pander** to a person's desires is to indulge and tolerate their weaknesses, to make unnecessary allowances for their vices. The verb 'to pander' comes from an earlier noun, 'pander' or 'pandar', which was popularised by William Shakespeare. In *Much Ado about Nothing* (1598), Benedick refers to the Trojan hero Troilus as 'the first employer of pandars'. At that time, a 'pandar' was basically a pimp, but Shakespeare's reference is also a play on words: Troilus, in both *Troilus and Cressida* by Shakespeare (1602) and *Troilus and Criseyde* by Chaucer (*c.*1385), employs his older friend Pandarus (or Pandare) as a go-between in his courtship of Cressida. This is where the word comes from.

According to Greek mythology, the original Pandarus was an energetic warrior who famously broke the truce between the Trojans and the Greeks by wounding Menelaus, the king of Sparta. In Homer's *Iliad*, an account of the Trojan Wars, Pandarus is portrayed as a hero among his people, but by Chaucer's time he had developed into a more matronly character, whose main task is to bring the ill-fated young lovers together. Shakespeare's Pandarus is bawdier still, and more cowardly pimp than courageous warrior. The word 'pander' originally meant 'a go-between for lovers' (hence pimp), and to this day it still technically means 'to minister to the baser desires, appetites or motives of another'. So next time anybody accuses you of pandering to your children, trust me: you are not.

Pandemonium is a state of complete uproar, indiscipline and riotous behaviour. It was originally the setting for Satan's HQ in John Milton's *Paradise Lost* (1667), the epic poem that tells the tale of Adam and Eve's temptation and subsequent expulsion from the Garden of Eden. Milton has Satan's heralds proclaim 'a solemn council forthwith to be held at Pandemonium, the high capital of Satan and his peers'. He had constructed the word based on the Greek *pan*, 'all', and *daimon*, 'demon'.

By the beginning of the nineteenth century, the word 'pandemonium' was being used to describe the venue of any lawless and riotous assembly, of which there were plenty at the time in London alone. By the middle of that century, it began to appear as a description of the uproar itself, rather than the place in which it took place.

A **heckler** is a person who can be found loudly interrupting a performance or speech with what he or she assumes to be hilarious or relevant commentary. The original hecklers were to be found in the textile industry, in which 'heckling' involved straightening out and removing the impurities from flax fibres, prior to spinning and weaving into linen, using a special combing device. And it was the hecklers of the politically militant Scottish city of Dundee who in the early nineteenth century developed the delicate art of **heckling** as we know it today. In the factory, the senior heckler, possibly the only literate one present, would read out the day's news while the others toiled at their looms, shouting out their particular opinions and getting embroiled in furious debate with fellow workers.

By the nineteenth century, heckling had become a largely tolerated part of popular theatre performances: some vaudeville shows even had heckling written into the script. More recently, *The Muppet Show* famously featured two grumpy old hecklers, Conrad Waldorf and Jerry Statler, while any stand-up comedian worth his or her salt has had to deal with the odd heckler over the years. Billy Connolly is a master, once telling a heckler, 'You should get an agent, pal, instead of sitting there in the dark handling yourself.' The brilliant Bob Monkhouse knew how to deal with them too, once firing back at one particularly irritating member of the audience: 'Half a million sperm and yours had to win.'

But the best responses to unwanted interruptions are usually off-the-cuff political ones that cannot be rehearsed.

Nancy Astor, the first woman to sit as a Member of Parliament, once challenged Winston Churchill with the words: 'Winston, if I were your wife I would poison your coffee.' To which Churchill famously retorted: 'Madam, if I were your husband I would drink it.' Or take the celebrated riposte of Labour politician Dennis Healey, during a debate in Parliament in June 1978, in which he likened criticism by Conservative minister Geoffrey Howe – the mildest of hecklers – to 'being savaged by a dead sheep'.

In the sporting arena there have been some great one-liners too. Cricketer Ian Botham once came up with a quick response when Australian batsman Rodney Marsh tried to put him off his stride with a well-aimed heckle. 'How's your wife and my kids?' Marsh taunted. 'The wife's fine,' Botham replied coolly, 'but the kids are retarded.' (See also BARRACKING, LUDDITE.)

Jumbo is a word we associate with anything of huge scale. We talk of **jumbo-sized** packets of crisps or **jumbo jets**, and use it as an affectionate NICKNAME for an elephant. And it is to a real-life elephant that we owe the expression.

The original Jumbo was a huge African bush elephant born in 1861 in the French Sudan, now Mali. As a youngster, he was taken to the Jardin des Plantes in Paris and exhibited there until 1865, before being transferred to London Zoo, where he became famous by giving rides to thousands of children. His keepers there called him Jumbo, borrowing the word from the Swahili *jambe*, 'chief'. Jumbo was quite the sensation at a time when most people had never encountered a twelve-foot, seven-ton beast, let alone had the chance to ride on one.

Such was his popularity that, when the zoo announced he was up for sale in 1882, over 100,000 schoolchildren wrote to Queen Victoria begging her not to allow him to leave. The old queen, with her customary consideration of her subjects, ignored them all and sold Jumbo for £10,000, approximately £4 million in today's money, to the legendary circus owner P. T. Barnum, producer of the 'Greatest Show on Earth'. To misquote Oscar Wilde in reference to the queen: 'If this is the way she treats her subjects [originally 'prisoners' – meaning himself, before being carted off to Reading Gaol], she doesn't deserve to have any.'

Jumbo embarked upon a three-year tour across America, thrilling the crowds wherever he went, but on a visit to Ontario in 1885 he was hit by a steam train and died. Some reports of the time claimed he died saving the life of a young elephant called Tom Thumb, of which there is absolutely no evidence, but it didn't do the legend of the world's most famous animal any harm. Alas, his work didn't end there: the unscrupulous Barnum had his hide stuffed and continued to tour with him for the next four years.

After Jumbo was finally retired in 1889, he spent almost a century on display at Tufts University in Boston,

Massachusetts, but a fire in 1975 destroyed the building and the great chief himself.

Blockbuster, meaning a massive bestseller, can be applied to either a book or a film. Some in the entertainment industry believe the word was first used in theatreland to describe a play that proved so successful in one venue that all the other theatres on the block were driven out of business, or went bust. But that is unlikely. What *is* likely is the word emerged during the Second World War, when it was used by American servicemen to describe their largest high-explosive bombs, which could destroy a whole block with just one direct hit.

This slang term was picked up by journalists of the time, who would use it in their reports from the frontline or to describe a bombing raid. The first true 'blockbuster', in the sense of box-office hit, was probably *Gone with the Wind* in 1939, but it was not until the release of *Jaws* in 1975 that the notion of a 'summer blockbuster' went mainstream. It's an ironic etymology, really, given that when a film is a spectacular flop, it is generally referred to in the States these days as having **bombed**.

Zombies are fictional characters, corpses that are terrifyingly brought back to life and wander around in a trance-like state. Used figuratively, the word denotes someone who appears lifeless and totally lacking in energy. Rather like a student on a weekend morning. Although they enjoy a long and colourful history, zombies as we know them were first introduced to the American public as recently as 1929, with the publication of a novel called *The Magic Island* by William B. Seabrook (1884–1945), a globetrotting, alcoholic, cannibalistic, sadomasochistic journalist.

Seabrook, a friend and associate of Aleister Crowley, the English occultist famously described by his mother as the 'Great Beast', shared the latter's passion for devil worship and the occult. Following his time spent among the Bedouin people of the Arabian Peninsula, his previous novel, *Adventures in Arabia* (1927), introduced whirling dervishes and devil worshippers to a goggle-eyed public. The book was successful enough to enable Seabrook to spend some time living in Haiti, where he studied the previously unrecorded folklore of that country while indulging his own passion for voodoo.

Although *The Magic Island* introduced the word 'zombie' to the American public, it was the succession of zombie-related films that followed in the 1940s, including *King of the Zombies* and *I Walked with a Zombie*, that put a face to this terrifying creature. It would be another twenty years until the English rock band the Zombies, who sadly looked nothing like the namesakes, scored a succession of hit singles in both the UK and America and brought the word to a wider audience. Then, in 1968, the cult horror movie *Night of the Living Dead* featured zombies in the ghoulish incarnation we know and love today. But where did the word come from in the first place?

West Africa appears to be the answer, and the snake god Zombi – a word related to the Kikongo *zumbi*, 'fetish', and the Kimbundu *nzambi*, 'god' – part of the voodoo cult that was transported to the West Indies and America with the African slaves in the seventeenth and eighteenth centuries. In the Southern states of America (see DIXIELAND) the belief was that the zombie had the power to enter a human corpse and bring it back to life, which is close to our understanding of what zombies do, although in Haiti, where Seabrook drew his influences, zombies are the bodies of the dead who have been brought back to life by the voodoo high priest. While numerous eyewitness accounts 'prove' that these reanimations took place, sceptics insist that living people were heavily drugged by the priests so as to appear half dead.

Although **jazz** has been used for around a century to describe the music that was born in New Orleans and quickly spread up the Mississippi River in the early 1900s before reaching Chicago (see DIXIELAND), nobody is quite sure how the word evolved. It had entered Californian slang by 1912 and was used – often as a synonym for 'oomph' or 'pep' – in San Francisco newspaper articles in 1913, but when it was first applied to the music remains obscure.

In 1924, American author Edwin DuBose Heyward

(1885–1940) published *Jasbo Brown and Selected Poems*, the title poem featuring an itinerant black musician who travels along the Mississippi and eventually settles in the Chicago cabarets. The name cropped up again the following year when George Brooks wrote a song called 'Jazzbo Brown from Memphis Town', which was regularly performed by Bessie Smith (1894–1937), heralded as the 'Empress of the Blues'. Then, in 1935, George Gershwin premiered his opera *Porgy and Bess* – based on a novel by DuBose Heyward – in which a character called Jasbo Brown plays the piano in a famous scene commonly referred to as 'Jasbo Brown Blues', which culminates with the classic song 'Summertime'.

But despite 'jazz' being selected by the American Dialect Society as the 'Word of the Twentieth Century', and the considerable research that has been carried out on its origins, no real-life Jasbo or Jazzbo Brown has ever been traced. Of course, this is no proof against an itinerant musician named Jasbo Brown having worked his way in towns along the Mississippi at the turn of the twentieth century: if anything, the use of the variant spellings by DuBose Heyward and Brooks suggests the name had travelled by word of mouth. So raise a glass with me to the real founder of jazz, Jasbo Brown, because I have a feeling somebody will find evidence of him some day.

Dixieland is both a place and a style of music. The area most JAZZ fans associate with Dixieland music is the group of Southern states below the Mason–Dixon Line, a borderline surveyed in the 1760s by Charles Mason and Jeremiah Dixon to settle a boundary dispute between various states and considered, until the abolition of slavery a century later, to mark the division between the slave states of the South and the free ones of the North. It was around this time too that the Southern states acquired the NICKNAME **Dixie** or 'Dixieland', which, according to one theory, may derive from 'Dixon', the surname of the surveyor, or, according to another, could be from *dix* (the French for 'ten') in reference to the ten-dollar notes or 'dixies' issued by banks in French-speaking parts of Louisiana. Whatever the case, it was thanks to the popular nineteenth-century song 'Dixie' by Daniel Emmett, which includes the line 'Away down south in Dixie', that fixed 'Dixie' and 'Dixieland', to mean the Southern states, in people's minds.

The distinctive music of this area travelled on paddle steamers up the Mississippi around the turn of the twentieth century, before spreading to Chicago, where it became particularly popular among the white musicians of the Windy City. The turning point came in March 1916, when a group led by drummer Johnny Stein played a set at Schiller's Café, Chicago, adopting the style they had heard from travelling Southern musicians. What was originally billed as Stein's Dixie Jass Band and then just the Dixie Jass Band went on to create a sensation in New York, where it was billed as the Original Dixieland Jass Band. Within a few months, the New Orleans style of jazz had swept through New York and Chicago. Following the release of the band's million-selling hit record in 1917, the word 'Dixieland' was firmly established as a way of describing Southern jazz music for Northern white men. Many of the later (and greater) Dixieland musicians were Southern and black – Louis Armstrong, for example – but 'Dixieland' remains largely associated with music from Dixieland played by white musicians of the North.

Boogie-woogie is an up-tempo style of piano-based blues music that evolved from JAZZ in the Southern states of America in the 1930s. The word comes from the inter-war years, when it became common for jazz musicians to hold what were known as 'rent parties', lively occasions where musicians would gather together and play while a hat was passed round to raise money for their weekly rent. Thousands of black musicians migrated from New Orleans to New York during this period, looking for work in the theatre pits or as street musicians. They mainly congregated in Harlem and started up their own rent parties, which played a vital part in the popularisation of jazz and blues in the north of the country. Some of the jazz and boogie-woogie legends such as Fats Waller, Count Baisie and Duke Ellington all honed their skills at rent parties, which were known as 'skiffles' or 'boogies' back home in New Orleans.

In December 1928, Alabama musician Clarence Smith, better known as Pinetop Smith, famously established the 'boogie-woogie' sound with the release of his popular rent-party song 'Pinetop's Boogie Woogie', which came with dance instructions included. Although Pinetop died the following year, his legacy was assured in 1938, when Tommy Dorsey and his Orchestra released their big-band version of Pinetop's song, which became an instant hit and sold over 5 million copies.

But what does 'boogie-woogie' actually mean? Well, there are four regional African words that might provide the origin of the word. The first is the West African *bogi*, pronounced 'boogi', which translates as 'to dance'. Then there is the Mandingo word *booga* and the Hausa word *boog*, both of which translate as 'to beat' (as in beating a drum), and finally the Congolese *mbuki mvuki*, an exhortation to throw off your clothes and dance. The word 'boogie', without the 'woogie', was a common slang word from the mid-nineteenth century, and the 'Boogie Man' made his first appearance in 1880 as the title of a piece of music.

SCIENCE AND NATURE

The **gadget**, an undefined mechanical device, is the older brother of the **gizmo** and the **widget**. Originally a nautical term, it first appeared in the 1870s. One of the earliest instances of 'gadget' in print was in Robert Brown's 1886 book *Spunyarn and Spindrift: A Sailor Boy's Log of a Voyage Out and Home in a China Tea-Clipper*, in which the boy of the title notes: 'Then there are the names of all the other items on board a ship. I don't know half of them yet; even the sailors sometimes forget, but if the exact name of anything they want happens to slip from their memory they call it a chicken-fixing, a gadget, a gill-guy, a timmy-noggy or a wim-wom.' Other etymologists, meanwhile, believe it was the French company Gaget, Gauthier & Cie − responsible for much of the iron framework used in the construction of the Statue of Liberty in the 1880s − that invented the word to describe various small custom-made pieces they had to design or improvise. Which sounds vaguely plausible except that there is little evidence to back it up.

It is, however, possible that there is a French connection. *Gâchette* has been used over the years to describe different parts of a firing mechanism, and the French can also claim *gagée*, a dialect word for a tool. Today gadgets tend to be the latest must-have technical product for showing off among one's peers: iPads rather than, say, spanners.

The **widget** was originally exactly the same thing, first recorded during the 1920s in America to describe a 'small gadget'. In the 1990s, however, the widget found a permanent home of its own when it was applied to the small device fitted into beer cans to maintain a creamy, frothy head.

Finally, the **gizmo** was introduced into the English language during the Second World War by US Marines. Sadly their precise inspiration is lost to history, but the word seems originally to have meant 'thingamajig'. As an article of November 1942 in *Leatherneck*, 'Magazine of the Marines', reveals: 'When you need a word for something in a hurry and can't think of one, it's a gizmo.'

The verb to **google** is one of the newest entries into the English language. We use it as a generic term for an internet search, even if we happen not to be using the search engine it is named after (see also YAHOO). But how did the founders of Google arrive at what is now one of the largest brand names on the planet?

Making his debut in 1919 in a cartoon strip called 'Take Barney Google, F'rinstance', which ran on the sports pages of the *Chicago Herald and Examiner*, Barney Google was a little chap with big eyes who was fond of boxing and horse racing. In 1924, cartoonist Billy DeBeck introduced a new character, a racehorse called Spark Plug, which lead to a huge increase in the popularity of the strip. Having gone national, Barney Google then went global, appearing across twenty-one countries by the mid-1930s. His slangy catchphrases included 'sweet mama', 'horsefeathers' and 'heebie-jeebies', and he is also thought to be the origin of the expression **googly-eyed**.

Such was the popularity of Barney Google by 1940 that, when mathematician Edward Kasner asked his nine-year-old nephew to suggest a name for the figure 10 followed by 100 zeros, the boy decreed it should be a **googol**. It was this word for an almost infinite number that Larry Page and Sergei Brin had in mind when they named their company in 1998.

Gabriel Daniel **Fahrenheit** (1686–1736) was a Polish-born Dutch physicist and engineer of German descent. He was just fifteen years old when both his parents died after eating poisonous mushrooms, and he was sent to Amsterdam to learn business and trade. But the young Fahrenheit was only interested in natural science and so began his studies in that field, learning about thermometers from the Danish astronomer Olaus Roemer, who was experimenting with them for meteorological purposes. Fahrenheit developed the first alcohol thermometer in 1709 and in 1724 he published a paper that defined an accurate temperature scale for the first time in history.

Meanwhile, over in Sweden, a certain Anders **Celsius** (1701–44) was busy growing up. His father was the professor of astronomy at the Uppsala University, a role Anders took on in 1730. In 1736, he took part in the expedition to Lapland that verified Newton's theory that the earth was flatter at the two poles and therefore not perfectly round. But he is best remembered for the scientific paper he published in 1742, which simplified Fahrenheit's principle by proposing 100° as the freezing point of water and 0° as the boiling point. Celsius's 100-point scale was obviously easier to understand than Fahrenheit's 180-point predecessor, although fellow Swedish scientist Carl Linnaeus made it even easier in 1744, the year of Celsius's death, by reversing the scale. The Celsius scale is gradually gaining acceptance – albeit grudgingly in most English-speaking countries – as the most practical measure of temperature.

The strange word **nth**, as used in the expression 'to the nth degree', indicates an unspecified high number. 'To the nth degree' literally means 'to the furthest extent possible'. It comes from the mathematical use of 'n' to denote an indefinite number. There is no limit to the nth degree. (See also UMPTEEN, X, X-RAY.)

Technically a **blizzard** is regarded as a snowstorm with winds blowing at over thirty-five miles per hour and visibility of less than a quarter of a mile for three consecutive hours. Anything less than that is, presumably, a mere snowstorm. The first recorded use of the word, in the civilised world at least, was during the brutal American winter of 1880–81, when the entire country was crippled for months. New York's *Nation* magazine noted: 'The hard weather has called into use a word which promises to become an Americanism, namely "blizzard". It designates a storm (of snow and wind) that men cannot resist away from shelter.' In other words: nobody goes outside in such weather.

The earliest record of the word in print, spelt 'blizard', is said to come from the *Northern Vindicator* of Estherville, Iowa, in its edition of 23 April 1870. The oft-repeated story among amateur etymologists is that the word was the invention of a colourful local named 'Lightnin' Ellis', who had coined it while hanging around the local newspaper office in an effort to keep warm, and that it was later picked up by the local baseball team which subsequently changed its name to 'The Blizzards'. Many years later, elderly locals who remembered Ellis were apparently quoted in the local press as saying: 'Ellis often used unusual words and "blizzard" has always been associated with him.'

But I am suspicious of this legend for three reasons. The first is that I have never found any other reference to 'Lightnin' Ellis' except in relation to this story. No one else has ever heard of him, elderly local or otherwise. Secondly, the only record I can find of a Blizzards baseball team is an under-fifteens side from Minnesota, whose first tournament was in 2007. There were no Blizzards listed with the National Association of Base Ball Players, the governing body, in 1870. The final small but clinching clue is that the word could not have appeared in the *Northern Vindicator* of Estherville on 23 April 1870, because there was no edition of the paper that day.

Estherville's claim doesn't really matter either way, though, because the word seems to have been in circulation well before 1870. The *Dictionary of Americanisms* included the word in both 1859 and 1861, quoting as its source the diary of an army captain stationed at Fort Leavenworth in Kansas. Prior to that, the King of the Wild Frontier, Davy Crockett, is believed to have used 'blizzard' twice in his accounts of the Texas Revolution of the mid-1830s, first to describe a shotgun blast and then a severe snowstorm.

Assuming for a moment that this story is true, it is quite likely that Crockett was misusing a word picked up from the German settlers fighting alongside him, who would have known 'lightning' as *Blitz*. Incidentally, if your nan is still alive, ask her if she knows why we called the German bombing of London during the Second World War 'the Blitz'. The answer is that we didn't: *they* did. The Blitz Krieg, to give it its full title, translates as 'lightning war'. On second thoughts, maybe don't remind your grandmother about that after all.

Groundhog Day is used, particularly in America and Britain, to denote a day that seems to repeat itself endlessly, or more generally a task that needs to be repeated many times until it is accomplished. The original Groundhog Day was a custom celebrated by German immigrants in Pennsylvania in the nineteenth century, linked to a folklore belief that a groundhog – also known as a woodchuck, a type of ground squirrel – would emerge from its burrow on the first day of spring to check the weather. If it was too cold he would remain underground, popping up again periodically until it was warm enough to emerge properly. The Irish have a similar festival known as Imbolc or St Brigid's Day – originally a pagan festival linked to the goddess Brigid before she was made respectable by being canonised – which is generally celebrated on the first day of February.

Groundhog Day as a modern–day concept was first alluded to in 1841, when James Morris, a shopkeeper from Berks Country, Pennsylvania, noted in his diary for February: 'Last Tuesday, the 2nd, was Candlemas Day on which, according to the Germans, a Groundhog peeps out of his winter quarters and if he sees his own shadow, he pops back in for another six weeks' nap. But if the day is cloudy he remains out as the weather is moderate.' The custom remained relatively unknown outside German-American communities until as recently as 1993, when the film *Groundhog Day*, starring Bill Murray, became a box-office hit. Murray, the central character, is forced to relive the same day over and over again until he learns to be less selfish. The film led to the word being used to describe anything that has to be repeated many times before being achieved satisfactorily.

When something is said to happen once in a **blue moon** it isn't going to happen very often. The inference is that it never will. This has nothing to do with the colour of the moon changing on rare occasions due to smoke or dust particles on the surface, although this has been known to happen – notably following the eruption of Krakatoa in 1883, when the moon looked blue for nearly two years.

But the origin of our phrase is much simpler than that and can be traced back to the lunar cycles. We all know that every year there is one full moon every MONTH, yet what we don't all know is that these twelve full moons have individual names: the Harvest Moon, the Hunter's Moon, the Hay Moon and so on. But approximately seven times in every nineteen years – which is a fancier way of saying 'once every two and three-quarter years' – there are thirteen full moons, since the lunar and calendar cycles don't quite match up. This means that for one month in every thirty-three or so there are two full moons. The 'spare' moon doesn't have a formal name but has traditionally been listed as 'blue' in the influential *Farmers' Almanac*, published annually in Maine since 1818.

An **agnostic** is a person who regards the existence of God as unprovable – which, given the widespread influence of modern science, should be just about everybody. As with any mystery, the onus of proof should always rest with whoever claims something to be true; it should be nobody's responsibility to prove that it does not exist or did not happen. But I digress. An agnostic accepts that a claim cannot always be proven and acknowledges that many claims cannot be unproven either.

The word was invented by the English biologist Thomas Huxley (1825–95) to describe his own beliefs. A vocal supporter of Charles Darwin's theory of evolution, he nevertheless recognised that the idea of there being no God at all was too unpalatable for most to contemplate. Realising the need for a third way, some middle ground that would gradually bring people round, he formulated the concept of agnosticism. It was at the inaugural meeting of the Metaphysical Society in Clapham, south London, in 1869, that he outlined the idea, explaining to the audience, which was largely made up of prominent clergymen and members of the church, that 'Agnosticism is not a creed but a method, the essence of which lies in the vigorous application of a single principle. Positively the principle may be expressed as in matters of intellect: do not pretend conclusions are certain that are not demonstrated or demonstrable.'

Huxley, who believed everybody should be agnostic until scientific proof could be found, or knowledge improved, invented his new word by borrowing from the Greek language: *a* means 'not' and *gnostos* means 'known'. Hence 'agnostic': 'not known'.

The use of the letter **X** to signify something unknown (see also NTH, UMPTEEN) was first suggested by the French philosopher and mathematician René Descartes (1596–1650), who used the first three letters of the alphabet for known quantities and the last three for any unknowns in his pioneering work *La Géométrie* (1637). In this work, Descartes proposed that algebra and geometry could be united (they were separate subjects before), with geometric shapes being expressed in the form of algebraic equations. All very groundbreaking except that, in the process, he managed to confuse every remedial maths and science student for the next 400 years. 'X to the power of four'? What on earth does that mean?

Like many of the great medical innovations and discoveries, the **X-ray** was happened upon by chance. Wilhelm Röntgen

(1845–1923) was a German physicist who studied mechanical engineering at the University of Zurich and went on to become professor of agriculture at the University of Würzburg in 1875. In November of that year, Röntgen was carrying out a series of experiments relating to cathode rays, which had recently been identified by another German scientist, Johann Hittorf (1824–1914). Röntgen was studying the external effects of these rays when they were passed through a vacuum in a glass tube, and he noticed that any fluorescent surface nearby would become luminous, even when shielded from the direct light.

He put the tube into a light-tight black cardboard box, turned off all the lights in his laboratory and began a series of experiments. Each time, he noticed a faint shimmering of light across the room. He struck a match to investigate and discovered that the light had been emitted from a screen painted with barium platinocyanide, which he had been intending to use for something else entirely. He began placing objects of various densities between the screen and the cathode rays and saw the bones of his hand appear on the screen without their usual covering of flesh.

Still unsure of exactly what type of ray was causing this new phenomenon, Röntgen named his new discovery after the mathematical term commonly applied to anything unknown: 'X' (see under its own entry). Within two weeks, Röntgen had taken the first ever *X-Strahl* ('X-ray') of his wife's hand; upon seeing her own skeleton, Frau Röntgen became faint and declared, 'I have just seen my own death.' Very soon the scientific community was referring to this new discovery as 'Röntgen rays', a name by which they are still known in many countries, although the man himself disapproved and insisted instead on them being called X-rays.

A **glitch** is a minor setback or fault, originally electrical, that is difficult to trace. Generally thought to be of unknown origin, the word seems to have passed into American English, having come, according to the *Random House Book of American Slang*, either from the Yiddish *gletshn*, 'to slip and slide', or the German *glitschen*, meaning much the same. Either way, the modern use of the word is usually associated with the American space programme of the early 1960s. In 1965, *Time* magazine defined 'glitch' as 'a spaceman's word for irritating disturbance'. Well, we all have our own words for 'irritating disturbance', don't we? And if the neighbour's dog won't stop barking, I'm sorely tempted to use one right now.

The word **blaze** (as in 'mark') entered the English language in the seventeenth century via the Middle Low German *bles*, 'white mark', which is also related to the word 'blemish'. In equestrian parlance, 'blaze' is another name for the white mark (or 'star') on a horse's forehead, while the practice among pioneers of marking a tree with a knife or sword in order to indicate a route is the origin of the phrase 'blazing a trail' and hence the word **trailblazer**.

The other kind of blaze – of a raging fire, or eyes burning with jealousy – comes from the Old English *blaese*, 'bright fire', which is also of Germanic origin (see also BLAZER).

Until the tragic events of Boxing Day 2004, any particularly huge wave that crashed into the shoreline was generally known as a tidal wave. But that phrase couldn't quite sum up the 100-foot-high body of water caused by an earthquake beneath the Indian Ocean, which killed an estimated 230,000 people across fourteen Southeast Asian countries. At the time, the word **tsunami** was virtually unheard of, unless you happened to be a fan of the Manic Street Preachers, and it doesn't even appear in the 2004 edition of the *Oxford Dictionary of Word Histories*. Even so, by 27 December that year, it had become a household word across the world.

Tsunamis, or 'tsunami wave trains', to give them their more technical name, can be traced back a long way in human history. In the fifth century BC, the Greek historian Thucydides was the first to suggest they were caused by ocean earthquakes. In his scroll (they didn't really have books in those days) *The History of the Peloponnesian War* (426 BC), he radically argued: 'The cause, in my opinion, of this phenomenon must be found in the earthquake. At the point where its shock has been the most violent the sea is driven back and suddenly recoils with double the force, causing the inundation. Without an earthquake I do not see how such an accident could happen.'

Since then, the country most affected by tsunamis has been Japan, which has suffered almost 200 of them since records began, the most powerful to date being the one that occurred in March 2011. As a result of the country's unfortunate association with this type of natural disaster, the word 'tsunami' is taken from the Japanese language: *tsu* means 'harbour' and *nami* means 'wave'.

It is traditionally claimed that the original Roman **calendar** – from the Latin *kalendae*, 'first day of the month', and the day on which accounts were due – was created by Romulus, the mythical founder of Rome, in around 738 BC. His year, based upon the ancient Greek lunar calendar, was made up of 304 days divided into ten months, each one lasting from one full moon to the next. One lunar cycle was called a *monath* (from *mona*, the 'moon') by the Anglo-Saxons, hence **month**.

The first of these was the beginning of the growing season, now known as **March** but originally named Martius, after Mars, the Roman god of war and guardian of all things agricultural. The second month of the year was called Aprilis, now **April**, which the Roman scholar Varro claimed was inspired by the Latin *aperire*, 'to open', in reference to the buds of flowers and trees beginning to unfold at that time of the year. The third month of the Roman calendar was known as Maius, hence **May**, in honour of the goddess Maia, who represented fertility and growth and whose annual festival was held at that time of year. Junius, or **June**, is the fourth month of the original calendar, named after Juno, goddess of marriage and wife of Jupiter. Just as now, June was considered a good month for a wedding, and not only because there was less risk (in Rome at least) of it being cold and wet. In Roman times, the first half of the month was a time of religious purification and hence considered auspicious by those wanting to get hitched.

By the fifth month of the year, Romulus was obviously running out of inspiration, or goddesses, since it was originally called Quintilis, from *quintus*, 'fifth'. But in 44 BC the Roman Senate renamed the fifth month Julius, or **July**, to commemorate Julius Caesar, who, although he had been assassinated in March of that year, was born in the month of Quintilis. The sixth month of the calendar was simply called Sextilis, 'sixth', but the name was changed to Augustus, **August**, in 8 BC in honour of Emperor Augustus Caesar, the adopted son of the aforementioned Julius, his great-uncle. To explain why this was such a good idea, the Senate saw fit to issue a formal decree:

Whereas the Emperor Augustus Caesar, in the month of Sextilis, was first admitted to the consulate and thrice entered the city in triumph, and in the same month the legions from the Janiculum placed themselves under his command and in the same month Egypt was brought under the authority of the Roman People [which annoyed Cleopatra no end] and in the same month an end was put to the civil wars and for these reasons the said month has been most fortunate to this empire, it is hereby decreed by the Senate that the said month shall now be called Augustus.

But I'm jumping ahead a bit here. Back in the days when July and August were plain old 'fifth' and 'sixth', the names of the remaining months of the year were equally uninspiring, and they haven't changed since then: **September** means 'seventh', **October** 'eighth', **November** 'ninth' and **December** (you've guessed it) 'tenth'. Which left sixty-one days of winter that were not assigned to anything: they were simply the cold days when nothing much happened and the Romans kept warm while awaiting the new growing season in March.

But then it all became interesting again. Long before the Roman emperors who gave their names to July and August, there was a king of Rome called Numa Pompilius (753–673 BC), who decided to do something about these missing days by adjusting the solar and lunar years and introducing two new months. Following December, the first brand new month would be called Januarius, **January**, named in honour of Janus, the Roman god with two faces who could look back at the old year and ahead into the new one at the same time. This was followed by Februarius, **February**, named after Februa, a Roman festival of ritual purification held under the full moon during this period. The fact that Pompilius was by now running out of days is reflected in February's peculiar shortness.

And that is how it stayed for over 600 years, until Julius Caesar decided that the calendar had become increasingly out of line with the natural seasons and asked the astronomer Sosigenes of Alexandria to sort it out. It was he who recommended using the sun instead of the moon as a basis for calculation, introducing the leap year in order to balance the cycle and moving the beginning of the year from March to January. This new format was successfully adopted on 1 January 45 BC and named the Julian Calendar. And that is why the last four months of the year are named after numbers that don't correspond to their positions in the sequence of twelve months.

We take for granted the names of the days of the week, but they have surprisingly interesting stories behind them. **Monday** was called 'Monandaeg' – 'day of the moon' – by the Anglo-Saxons, and it is named after the moon in a great many languages. The Romans called it *dies lunae*, for instance, another 'day of the moon'. **Tuesday** has for millennia been known as the 'day of Mars' (after the Roman god of war) in a number of languages (*mardi* in French, *martes* in Spanish), but the Anglo-Saxons, heavily influenced at the time by their Norse occupiers the Vikings, opted for 'Tiw's day' in honour of Tiw, the Norse god of war and law. **Wednesday** is another one with a strong Norse connection. Known as 'Wodensdaeg' by the Anglo-Saxons, the middle day of the week celebrates the chief of the Norse gods, Odin (Wodan in Old High German). In many other European languages, Wednesday is associated with the god Mercury, hence *mercredi* in French and *miércoles* in Spanish.

And so we're over the hump of the week and into **Thursday**. Originally called 'Thunresdaeg' – 'Thunor's day', in honour of the Norse god of thunder, storms and lightning, aka Thor – the name developed via Thunderday and Thuresday into Thursday. In the non-Norse-inspired countries, the day is named after Thor's Roman counterpart, Jove: *jeudi* in French and *jueves* in Spanish. **Friday**, the most popular day of the week, was known to the Romans as the 'day of Venus', goddess of love, and it still is to our Continental cousins: *vendredi* in French and *viernes* in Spanish. Venus's equally lovely Norse equivalent was Frige, hence Friday in English and *Freitag* in German.

At last we've reached the weekend, which kicks off with what the Romans named the 'day of Saturn' in the second century AD, in honour of the planet they believed controlled the first hour of what was at that time the last day of the week. To the Anglo-Saxons this was 'Saeturnesdaeg', now of course **Saturday**. And finally we come to Sunday, for many centuries the first day of the week and traditionally, according to the Christian faith, the day of the Sabbath or the day of rest. Although many languages renamed the day in honour of God (*dies Dominica* in Latin, hence *dimanche* in French, *domingo* in Spanish, *domenica* in Italian), others retained the good old pagan connection with the sun. The

Welsh have their *dydd Sul*, the Dutch *zondag* and the Scandinavians *søndag* or *söndag*, while the Anglo-Saxons had 'Sunnandaeg', now **Sunday**, 'day of the sun'.

The English word **week**, incidentally, comes from the Old English *wice*, meaning 'to move, turn or change', a reference to the ending of one period of days every Saturday.

TOYS, GAMES AND SPORTS

The game of **conkers** has been popular with generations of schoolboys for hundreds of years, as the scars on my knuckles still attest. We used to think the word had something to do with 'conqueror', in that there were inevitably winners and losers, but in fact it comes from 'conch-shells', or rather snail shells, which were once bashed against each other until one of them smashed and a winner was declared. When demand for 'conkers' began to outstrip supply – or perhaps when little boys realised smashing snails against each other wasn't terribly nice – horse chestnuts became the more common weapon of choice.

Checkmate is nowadays most often used in a business context, particularly in reference to thwarting the intentions of a rival. One company might hold a company 'in check' by stealing a valuable client, for example, or 'checkmate' it entirely by mounting a hostile takeover.

The word is of course derived from the game of chess, and is used to indicate that the winning player has managed to trap the opponent's king, rendering it useless and the game over. One of the oldest board games in history, chess has been enjoyed around the world for over 1,500 years, having originated in India and then spread through Persia into Europe.

The game was originally called *chaturanga*, which translates roughly as 'four military divisions', and players would cry '*shah mat*', 'the king is helpless', if they thought they had trapped an opponent's royal piece. As the game travelled across Europe during the tenth century, the cry of '*shah mat*' evolved into 'checkmate'.

Now, **golliwog** is a word that I am sure has my new editor already hovering over her 'delete' button. It has been the subject of heated debate over recent years, and not just over its exact origin. Golliwog was originally an African character in a children's picture book called *The Adventures of Two Dutch Dolls and a Golliwogg*, written by American author Bertha Upton and published in 1895. The book became a huge success and a worldwide golliwog craze followed. When in 1910 the British jam manufacturer John Robertson saw how many children were playing with the dolls, he developed the character Golly as a mascot for his company's jams and marmalades. Perhaps unbelievably, Golly was not retired from service until 2001.

The golliwog is often blamed for having generated an offensive word used to describe people of African descent, but perhaps wrongly as it turns out. It is thought by some that the term may in fact have evolved from the acronym applied to the overseas labourers employed across the British Empire, who were required to wear armbands bearing the initials WOGS: 'Working On Government Service'.

As for the name of Bertha Upton's original doll, this is thought to have been invented by the book's illustrator, Bertha's daughter Florence, who merged the words 'golly' and 'polliwog' (an American word for 'tadpole'). Others, meanwhile, and I am one of them, believe that the word developed after British soldiers returned from duty in Egypt bearing as a gift a popular children's toy from that country: a rag doll stuffed with black material, called a ghuliwog.

Given that Bertha Upton had immigrated to Britain in 1887 after the death of her husband, and when Florence was only fourteen, it is highly likely that the young artist would have known about ghuliwog dolls and may even have owned one herself. Whatever the origin of the word, however, the toy itself, a century later, began to be seen by many as a symbol of racism. In the mid-1980s, Ken Livingston's Greater London Council BOYCOTTED any product endorsed by a golliwog, and in 1988 the character disappeared from our television screens for ever. By 2007,

British police were seizing golliwogs from toyshops after complaints that the dolls were offensive.

But we live in an age of political correctness gone mad in which even the innocuous children's nursery rhyme 'Baa Baa Black Sheep' has been banned in many schools and replaced with 'Baa Baa Rainbow Sheep'. I kid you not. My advice is to take a look in your grandmother's loft and see if she is hiding her golliwog up there. If she is, don't report her; instead, hide the doll. It might be worth a lot of money one day.

A horse that is **cantering** is moving at a speed somewhere between a trot and a gallop. And the word is only ever used in association with horses; dogs and cats never canter, and neither do lions and elephants. When the Anglo-Saxons invaded the southern part of England in the fifth century, taking over cities and towns previously occupied by the retreating Roman Empire, they gave the major town of Durovernum Cantiacorum a new name, Cantwaraburg, which meant 'the town of the men of Kent'. It has since become known as Canterbury. Kent switched from paganism to Christianity at the end of the sixth century, largely thanks to a Benedictine monk called Augustine (later St Augustine), who had been sent over by Pope Gregory I for that very purpose, and Canterbury's place as the seat of the Christian church in England was established. (There is a point to all of this, I promise.)

A few centuries later, in 1170, Archbishop of Canterbury

Thomas à Becket was hacked to death at the altar of Canterbury Cathedral by four renegade knights from Henry II's court, who had supposedly taken the king's throwaway comment 'Will no one rid me of this turbulent priest?' quite literally. The cathedral became a shrine to the holy martyr almost immediately, with pilgrims travelling from all over England to visit the scene of the crime. One of the most famous pilgrimages to Canterbury, of course, is documented in Geoffrey Chaucer's *Canterbury Tales*, written at the end of the fourteenth century. The relaxed pace suitable for long-distance riding that would have been adopted by the Wife of Bath, the Knight and the many other real-life pilgrims later became known as a 'Canterbury gallop'.

The Sport of Kings (horse racing to you and me) became incredibly popular in Britain in the early eighteenth century, by which stage 'Canterbury gallop' was an established phrase. It was used outside the sport – carriage drivers, for instance, always travelled at a Canterbury gallop – but within the horse-racing community the expression was gradually abbreviated to 'Canterbury' and then 'canter', the word we still use today. I doubt this is quite what Pope Gregory I had in mind, however, when he sent Augustine over to Kent.

A **handicap** refers either to a disability or to a way of levelling the odds in a game or sport, especially golf or horse racing. The origin of the latter definition is believed to derive from 'hand in cap', a lottery or trading game that was very popular in seventeenth-century England. Pastimes may have been few and far between in those days, but gambling was just as prevalent. For those too low on the social scale to participate in horse racing, the 'Sport of Kings', hand in cap became a popular alternative, especially in London, in the coffee houses and on the street corners of the capital. As the great diarist of that age, Samuel Pepys, wrote on 18 September 1660: 'And here some of us fell to handicap, a sport I had never known before and that was very good.'

Hand in cap was a game played by two men, often traders, with a neutral referee. All three would put their hands into the referee's cap, each holding an unspecified amount of forfeit money. The referee would then announce a valuation, which could be either the value of an item presented for sale, the difference in value ('odds') between two items the players hoped to trade, or the odds of a sporting contest, such as prize fighting. Once the valuation had been announced, the two main players showed their assent or dissent by withdrawing their hands, each having either dropped the forfeit money into the cap (if he thought it an unfair deal) or kept hold of it (if he accepted the referee's price or odds). The forfeit money went to the referee if the opponents agreed with each other and to the assenting player if there was disagreement between them, with the balance of the transaction made up if a deal had been struck. The purpose of all this was to reward a fair valuation by the referee.

By the mid-eighteenth century this practice of evening

up the odds of a transaction was being used at horse-racing tracks across England, where it became gradually more common for race officials to 'handicap' a superior horse by adding weight to its saddle in an attempt to increase the chance of any horse winning (see also SANDBAGGER).

While the use of the word to describe a disabled person can conceivably have arisen via this notion of advantage versus disadvantage, the etymology for this definition is probably unrelated, however. The origin of the term is believed to be more recent, in fact, dating instead to the nineteenth century, when significant medical advances were made especially when it came to treating wounded soldiers, thereby greatly increasing their chances of survival when they would previously have perished on the battlefield. These men may have escaped with their lives, but their injuries still resulted in permanent disability in many cases, preventing them from taking up their former occupations when they returned home. In response to the number of incapacitated veterans of the Crimean War (1853–6), the British government made it legal for them to beg for money ('cap in hand') on the streets, as a result of which they became known as 'cap handy' or **handicapped**. The term was in standard use by 1915, when the government of the day introduced disability insurance for returning veterans of the First World War to discourage them from flooding into the cities with their caps in hand, which by then was deemed detrimental to public morale.

There are two types of **caddie** or **caddy**: one who carries your golf clubs around and the other in which your grandmother kept her tea leaves cool and dry.

The Cadets de Gascoigne were a French military unit made up entirely of the youngest sons of the Gascony aristocracy during the rule of Louis XIII (1601–43). The word *cadet* translates literally as 'little head' or 'inferior head', although 'junior' is the context in which it was used. The image of these dashing young aristocrats, who counted writer Cyrano de Bergerac among their number, appealed widely to the French public. Indeed, two centuries later, in 1844, Alexandre Dumas, author of *The Count of Monte Cristo*, began publishing a series of stories that later became *The Three Musketeers*, in which the musketeers of the title were also members of the Cadets de Gascoigne.

Because of the close military ties, known as the Auld Alliance, between England's historic enemies France and Scotland, many military terms were shared by the two armies during the late Middle Ages and beyond. Consequently, a 'caddie', as the Scots pronounced *cadet*, was a gentleman joining the army without a commission, with the intention of pursuing a military career. Over time, the word took on a wider definition, indicating any unskilled young man, or errand boy, who was looking for a day's work. Eventually caddies were employed only by golfers, thanks to the popularity of that game north of the border, and since the eighteenth century have had nothing more dashing or dangerous to do than carry a fat old man's golfing bags around. And that's not likely to have inspired any French novelists, is it?

But all of this has nothing to do with the tin in which your grandmother stored her tea, also called a 'caddy'. That word is thought to have evolved from the Southeast Asian measurement of weight called a *catty*. Approximately equivalent to one and a third pounds, the *catty* is a standard measure of tea, tons of which were imported into Britain on the tea clippers of the nineteenth century. (Incidentally, a 'teapoy', a three-legged occasional table upon which one might place a tray of tea, is not in fact named after the English national drink. The word is made up of the Hindi *ti*, 'three', and the Urdu *pai*, 'foot'.)

A **pundit** is supposed to be an expert on a subject. Every day various pundits appear on television, radio and all over our newspapers to air their opinion on matters ranging from football to politics, cookery to comedy. Given that so few of them come across as wise or even eloquent, you might be surprised to learn that, in India, a *pandit* is a Hindu scholar or 'learned man', well versed in the law, religion, the scriptures and Sanskrit. The word was brought back to England in the nineteenth century during the time of the Raj (see BUNGALOW) and is now used to describe any so-called expert or authority on just about any subject.

A **stickler** is somebody who insists on certain standards, however trivial, usually to the minor irritation of others. We have had sticklers since at least the twelfth century, when Geoffrey of Monmouth gave an account in his *Historia Regum Britanniae* of the Cornish hero Corineus's wrestling victory over the giant Gogmagog. Wrestling is still practised in Cornwall and the umpire goes by the old name of 'stickler' (from the Anglo-Saxon *stihtan*, 'to set in order') – traditionally there would be three of them watching each bout. By the sixteenth century, the definition of the word had become broader, to describe someone who 'arranges order' or 'upholds the rules', a pedant in other words.

The thoroughbred horses that are nowadays used in racing are cross-breeds of English mares and Arab horses imported to England around the turn of the eighteenth century. At the same time as horse racing was growing popular in England, it was also becoming something of a national pastime in Ireland, and the first **steeplechase** – literally a race from one church to another – was arranged in County Cork in 1752. The race was the result of a wager between Cornelius O'Callaghan and Edmund Blake as to which man owned the better horse, and it was run cross-country over the four miles between Buttevant and Doneraile. The modern steeplechase course has fences, ditches and other obstacles scattered along it to make it appear 'cross-country', but it doesn't replicate what supposedly happened at the end of the very first race: the winner rode straight into the church at Doneraile and down the aisle, just as the vicar was holding a funeral service.

Once something is (or has gone) **kaput**, it is of no further use to us. 'Kaput' was first recorded in use in England in around 1895, but it wasn't until after the First World War that it came into regular use, having been borrowed from the enemy soldiers. In German, *kaputt* literally means 'broken'. The Germans in turn borrowed their word from the French *capot*, which was a card-playing term meaning 'without tricks', although used in the sense that a player's hand was ruined, or bust.

Quiz nights are popular in pubs and clubs across the world, but it's heartening to find that the source of the word is Dublin. One evening in 1780, a theatre manager named Daly made a wager with his friends that he could introduce a brand new – and entirely meaningless – word to the English language. To make the bet more interesting, he added that he would achieve this within forty-eight hours. The bet was readily accepted and within hours Daly had chalked the letters Q-U-I-Z on doors and walls all over the city. Naturally the unusual-looking word became the talk of the town and newspapers were soon running competitions to determine its meaning. Daly won his bet because the word became associated with finding answers to questions, and indeed with people mulling over the 'quiz' question in inns and coffee houses, as they continue to do today. There is actually no hard evidence to support this story, but it's still a great pub fact, and one often repeated by trivia enthusiasts.

The history of the word **barracking** and indeed its definition have become confused over the years, which is hardly surprising since both Australia and Northern Ireland stake a claim to it.

We in the civilised English-speaking world understand the word 'barrack' to mean 'jeer' or 'make rude comments in an attempt to interrupt', but in the land down under, where the word actually originated in the 1870s, it means the exact opposite: 'to cheer and support'. The story goes that, in the mid-nineteenth century, supporters of the Victoria Barracks team at South Melbourne Cricket Ground would be greeted with howls and jeers of 'Here come the barrackers' by opposition supporters. It would seem that Australian sports fans regarded HECKLING the opposition as a show of support for their own team, which is how 'barrack' ended up meaning quite the opposite down under to what it does here, where barracking the opposition is just plain old barracking the opposition.

A separate Australian-based suggestion for the etymology of 'barrack' is that it comes from the ABORIGINE *barak*, 'banter', although the first recorded use of the word in print is in the sense of 'jeering and interrupting'. In a popular 1878 publication called *The Pilgrim: A Sensational Weekly Pamphlet*, printed in Sydney, we find: 'Douglas mumbled over a petition for the edification of the assembled roughs and larrikins, but was greeted with noisy insults and cries of "cheese your barracking and shut up".'

213

(**Larrikin** – or 'little Larry' – incidentally, used to mean 'mischievous youth' in Australia and New Zealand, but has since taken on the meaning of THUG.)

Meanwhile, in Northern Irish dialect, 'to barrack' is 'to brag', which is close enough to the modern meaning to be a credible alternative.

The famous old British **bulldog**, which actually began life as an English bulldog, doesn't get its name from the equally famous **bulldog spirit** it now represents, but instead from a charming pastime our ancestors called 'bull-baiting'.

One of the most popular blood sports of the seventeenth and eighteenth centuries, bull-baiting was as widely practised in London as the other more well-known blood sports cock-fighting and bear-baiting. Those who called themselves competitors in this grisly pursuit – which surely has to be up there on the British Wall of Shame alongside the creation of the Empire and the suppression of the Irish – would publicly torture a defenceless bull using dogs that had been specially bred to have an aggressive nature and a low centre of gravity. The bull, having been chained to a stake by the neck or leg, would have pepper blown into its nose to enrage it, and the dogs would then be set upon it, one at a time. The winner would be the dog that successfully attached its formidable jaws to the bull's snout, having carefully negotiated a pair of thrashing horns in the process.

Growing revulsion at this so-called sport during the late eighteenth century led to a bill for its suppression being introduced to Parliament in 1802, but incredibly it was defeated by thirteen votes. (It is important to remember that this happened at a time when the British upper classes and Members of Parliament were self-serving idiots – worse than now – and that they were the only people allowed to vote.) The Cruelty to Animals Act of 1835 finally banned the 'keeping of any pit or other place for baiting or fighting any bull, bear, dog or other animal'. So that was the animals sorted out, although they carried on being cruel to children, and the French, and many others, for another century.

Over time, the bulldog has developed into a non-aggressive and much-loved family pet, a proud national symbol rather than a reminder of the country's dubious past.

A **sandbagger** in a sporting context is a player who is deliberately underperforming in the run-up to a contest, in order to lull the opposition into a false sense of security. The word is now mainly used in motor racing, in which it is common practice for a team to save their true speed and performance for qualifying rounds or even the actual race.

Some etymologists believe the word comes from the street gangs of Victorian London, who would carry about a sock full of sand: harmless-looking enough until it was felt behind the ear. Others argue, meanwhile, that it was common practice to HANDICAP a horse with bags of sand, to slow it down in order to affect the outcome of a race that it might have been predicted to win.

But the real origin of 'sandbagger', and the practice of **sandbagging**, can be traced to the days when the qualifying system for motor races meant the fastest drivers began at the back of the grid, making for a more even and exciting race. In the days when racetrack safety consisted simply of placing sandbags in front of the spectators at dangerous corners, drivers trying to perform badly were able to drive at high speed but then deliberately misjudge a few corners, relying on the sand bags to slow them down without anybody necessarily noticing, thereby avoiding disqualification for cheating.

The word **shindig** was first recorded in the context of a large, noisy party in America in 1870, although the *Oxford English Dictionary* dates it to 1840 with the definition 'a kick in the shins'.

The rise of industrialisation meant that factory and mill workers needed footwear that was cheap, strong and easily available, and so the clog became a popular choice, particularly in Lancashire, where these shoes were worn from around 1835 until the end of the First World War. Clog fighting was not uncommon, either, becoming the traditional way to settle a dispute. Two opponents would kick each other until one submitted, while their fellow workers placed bets on the outcome. These fights would almost certainly have been noisy, rowdy affairs, entailing many vicious digs to the shins and quite possibly influencing the 'party' definition by the time these same workers migrated to America.

A second origin is suggested by the author and essayist Jerome K. Jerome, who uses the word 'shindy' in a passage from his *Idle Thoughts of an Idle Fellow* (1886): 'I always do sit with my hands in my pockets except when I am in the company of my sisters, my cousins, or my aunts; and they kick up such a shindy.' It seems clear from this that 'shindy' and 'shindig' – in the sense of a brawl – were the same word, or had at least evolved from the same origin. And that origin could well be the old Scottish game of shinty, or shinny. This is a cross between hockey and the Gaelic game of hurling, played with a hard ball and long curved sticks. Although 'shinty' appears only to have a coincidental similarity to the English word 'shin', it isn't hard to imagine the state of some of the shins at the end of a boisterous match. There was a good reason we called hockey 'hackey' at my school, I assure you: it literally was a shindig.

A **haymaker** is a boxing term for a giant punch, not dissimilar to a CORKER (in its original sense), swung from behind the shoulder and usually knocking an opponent out. It harks back to the days when the hay harvest was done by hand by farm labourers using a scythe, a long curved blade that was wielded from behind the shoulder. The haymaker would spend the harvest season out in the fields cutting hay with huge swinging strokes. No doubt he could also deliver a good punch down at the village tavern too when things became rowdy.

NICKNAMES AND INSULTS

Nicknames have been given to people since the days when surnames were very rare. To distinguish one 'John' from another, town and country folk alike would tack on to the end of their name their particular trade or a personal characteristic. So John the Ploughman could be found out in his field and John the Smith would be slaving over his hot forge, while John the Taffy was unfortunate enough to come from Wales. In the thirteenth century, this second name was called an 'eke-name', *eke* being the word for 'also', so it was the 'also' or 'other' name a person could be identified by. It is thought that, over time, 'eke-name' was mispronounced 'neke-name', hence 'nickname'.

Bumpkin, **yokel** and, in America, **hick** are all derogatory words used by city dwellers who consider themselves superior to their rural counterparts.

During the seventeenth century, when English was developing into a single national language instead of a number of regional dialects, the English and the Dutch were long-term military and trading rivals. The hostile English attitude towards the Dutch can be found in the diaries of Samuel Pepys, the great chronicler of his day. Typical entries might read: 'Several seamen came this morning and said they wanted to go and do all they could against the Dutch' and 'So to my home where my heart aches as the Dutch have burned our ships'. It was so common for the English to discuss the Dutch in a disparaging fashion that many of the insults in common parlance around this time entered the English language and are still in regular use over 300 years later. One of these words, 'bumpkin', was actually a Dutch word in origin: *bommekijn* or 'little barrel'. So the English were in effect calling their foe short, fat and empty.

In America, 'yokel' is applied to anybody living in a rural area, the word used in a similar way to 'hick' or 'redneck'. In England, it usually denotes a person from the West Country, conjuring up an image of someone in a white smock and straw hat, sucking on a piece of straw and drawing cider from a barrel into a toby jug while talking about tractors. Or is that just me?

The word 'yokel' is believed by some to derive from 'yoke', the harness used to connect a pair of oxen at the shoulders. Less convincing is the theory that it evolved from the Old English word for a green woodpecker, also called a yokel. Although they both reside in the country, I fail to see the connection between a woodpecker and my image of a yokel. More likely the word is a slight corruption of the Alemannic German word *jockel*, meaning 'fool'. Alemannic German is a mixture of dialects originating from various German tribes who inhabited wide areas between France and Italy and fought many wars with the Roman Empire between AD 250 and 380.

'Hick' is another word used in America to describe unsophisticated farming folk, specifically those living in the Deep South. For its origin we need to look to Andrew Jackson (1767–1845), the seventh president of the United States and the first to come from a humble, rural background. He was hugely popular throughout the Southern states (see DIXIELAND), having commanded the American forces at the Battle of New Orleans in 1815, where he convincingly defeated an invading British army attempting to capture this key Southern port. Known for his mental and physical strength, he was revered as 'tough Andrew Jackson' and later earned the NICKNAME 'Old Hickory' in a reference to his hard-as-wood nature. 'Tough as Old Hickory' became a well-known American phrase during the nineteenth century, and to this day people living in rural areas are still called 'hicks' – a name that was thought to be complimentary, to begin with at least.

Chatterbox is an affectionate term for those irritating people who love to share their news or wisdom with everyone they meet. Possibly related to 'clack-dish' – a box or dish for collecting coins that would be shaken loudly by beggars in the fifteenth century to encourage people to donate more money – the word was first recorded in its present form around 1770 and defined in the first edition of Grose's *Dictionary of the Vulgar Tongue* (1785) as 'one whose tongue runs twelve score to the dozen'. A similar expression, 'chatter-basket', was used in the nineteenth century to describe a 'prattling child', while 'chatter-broth' was, very appropriately, a term for the beverage shared to this day by those enjoying a good gossip – tea.

The **chattering classes**, incidentally, were first identified by the British satirical columnist Auberon Waugh. The expression is often used by political commentators as a derogatory term for politically active people who are considered to be on the fringes of popular influence and more likely to spread gossip than facts. Journalists working on local newspapers could well fall into this category, although the exact demographic of the 'chattering classes' remains something of a mystery. In 1999, *The Times Literary Supplement* printed a letter asking, 'Who are these chattering classes? This phrase, like PC, is now commonly used by lazy arrogant people to abuse the people and the ideas they don't like without having to justify their contempt.' A letter written, presumably, by a member of the chattering classes themselves. The one thing of which we can all be certain, however, is that none of us is a member: it's only ever other people.

There are various suggestions for the origin of the word **nincompoop**, which surprisingly is still in such common usage today that the Microsoft spellchecker doesn't pick up on it. So how did this word – usually applied to idiots and fools – evolve? To begin with, it is almost certainly not associated with the Latin phrase *non compos mentis*, meaning mentally incompetent or insane, as the great Dr Johnson would have us believe. First recorded in the 1670s, the word *poop* was widely used to describe a fool, and some etymologists have suggested that it was then combined with the French *nicodème*, 'simpleton'. I believe they are wrong, and not least because Nicodème is a relatively popular French boys' name that comes from the Greek *nikodemos*, 'victory of the people', and hence nothing to do with fools or idiots – except perhaps of the militant kind. It seems that we may remain in France, however, for the origin of 'nincompoop': the now obsolete phrase *nic à poux* (*poux* meaning 'lice' or 'nits') was a popular term of derision from the late 1500s.

Pipsqueak is thought by some to have been a NICKNAME given by British troops to incoming German shells during the First World War, 'squeak' being the noise they made as they flew overhead and 'pip' the sound of their explosion. And no, I'm not convinced by that either. Although British troops did have various nicknames for German artillery shells – 'whiz bang', 'coal box' and the 'flying sausage' (stop sniggering at the back, this is a serious matter) – 'pipsqueak' was not one of them.

The word does have First World War origins, however, and relates to three medals awarded to British troops who served between 1914 and 1918. Officially they were called the 1914 Star (later the 1914/1915 Star), the British War Medal and the British Victory Medal, but they were known more affectionately at the time as Pip, Squeak and Wilfred. In fact, they still are today among those with a knowledge of or interest in the Great War. But how did they acquire these odd nicknames?

After the fighting in Europe had eventually ended, the British newspaper the *Daily Mirror* began a long-running cartoon strip called 'Pip, Squeak and Wilfred', written by Bertram Lamb and illustrated by Austin B. Payne. The cartoon featured Pip the dog, Squeak, a penguin, and Wilfred the rabbit. In naming his first two characters, Lamb was inspired by Payne's wartime BATMAN, who was known for some reason as 'Pip-Squeak'. Such was the instant popularity of the cartoon strip that the three new service medals issued at around the same time acquired the nicknames Pip, Squeak and Wilfred. The transition to the modern meaning of 'pipsqueak' – a weak and insignificant person – presumably developed from the cute cartoon animals, however, rather than from the campaign medals.

A **whippersnapper** is a term your granddad might use to describe a cheeky and impish lad. (Or was that just my granddad?) One theory holds that the expression evolved in the nineteenth century on the ranches of the developing American Midwest, where it was used to describe the youngest farmhand, often a child too young to even ride a horse and whose only task was to 'snap the whip'. It is certainly plausible and there may be some truth in it, but the word was already in use by the upper classes in eighteenth-century England, as a derogatory term for beggars and thieves who idled on street corners and generally carried small whips. These dubious characters were known as 'snipper-snappers' or 'whipper-snappers', and were definitely to be avoided. (See also NIPPER.)

A **Luddite** is a person who is unable or unwilling to accept new and emerging technology – and in these fast-moving times there are more and more of us around. The original Luddites were aggrieved textile workers from Nottingham who, in 1811, began to protest against the introduction of factory machinery following the Industrial Revolution, which saw their prospects of employment drastically reduced.

They smashed over 200 industrial machines and burned down a number of mills, and the movement quickly spread to other parts of the country. At one stage, the British army was spending more resources on suppressing the Luddites than on dealing with Napoleon Bonaparte in the run-up to the Battle of Waterloo. The most active mob members were soon rounded up and brought to mass trial in York in 1812, as a result of which many were executed and hundreds more transported to Australia never to return (see POMMY), which should have been enough of a deterrent for anybody else.

The Luddites are commonly believed to have been led by a man called Ned Ludd, although they themselves tended to refer to him as King Ludd or General Ludd. It is quite possible that this fellow never existed, although there are stories about a Ned Ludd who, in 1779, supposedly smashed two knitting machines after being whipped for idleness. Real or fictional, he had become something of a folk legend among textile workers by the time of the Luddite movement of 1811–2, to the extent that even the wider public blamed Ned Ludd every time a stocking frame or weaving loom was destroyed. For a man who probably never existed in the first place, Ned certainly gave our language an excellent word. (See also HECKLER for a related one.)

Batty is used to mean 'eccentric and crazy', but usually in a harmless and loveable sort of way. It would seem that the word developed from the old expression 'to have **bats in the belfry**', which is a wonderfully batty English way of describing the harmlessly eccentric or even mentally challenged. To call a person 'bats' or 'batty' is a natural extension of this. But how did this expression come about in the first place?

There are suggestions that the phrase is rooted in the medical profession, specifically a William Battie MD (1704–76), an early psychiatrist and the esteemed author of *A Treatise on Madness* (1758). But Battie has competition from Batty – Fitzherbert Batty – an eminent barrister from Spanish Town, Jamaica, who was certified insane in London in 1839, an event that made the headlines.

It would be nice to be able to connect either of these characters to the expression, but in fact there is no real evidence of 'batty' being used before the turn of the twentieth century. By 1937, 'bats in the belfry' was certainly well enough known to be used as the title of a comic play by Diana Morgan and Robert MacDermot, whose cast in the first production in London included a young Charles Hawtrey of *Carry On* fame and, surprisingly, an equally young Vivien Leigh.

The expression was causing ripples of amusement across London at least twelve years before the play, however, as the essayist Stephen Graham explained in *London Nights* (1925): 'There is a set of jokes which are the common property of many comedians. You can hear them just as easily in Leicester Square as you can in Mile End Road. It strikes the unwanted visitor to the Pavilion as very original when Stanley Lupino says of someone, "He has bats in the belfry", as it is not always understood that the expression belongs to the music hall at large.'

It is generally accepted that the word **toff** and the associated expression **toffee-nosed** evolved from the 'tuft', or gold tassel, worn on the academic cap by titled undergraduates at Oxford and Cambridge universities during the nineteenth century. These students would characteristically turn their noses up at the likes of you and me, from which 'tuft-nosed' and then 'toff-nosed' developed. 'Toff' was in regular use by the 1930s, largely thanks to the crime and science-fiction writer John Creasey (1903–73), who published nearly sixty 'toff adventures' featuring an upper-class detective called the Honourable Richard Rollison, aka 'the Toff'.

While the snooty students and their famous hats are undoubtedly the source of the modern term, it could be that the Anglo-Saxon word *toforan*, meaning 'superior', contributed to its evolution – although it is quite unlikely that many working-class Victorians were familiar with the nuances of Anglo-Saxon.

A **ragamuffin** has been a ragged and scruffy person, usually a child, for a great many years. It first appeared in print in the allegorical late fourteenth-century poem *Piers Plowman* by William Langland, in which 'Ragamoffyn' appears as a devil or demon. Langland had most likely been inspired by the medieval word *ragman*, which meant 'the devil' (see also RIGMAROLE), although other etymologists have suggested the word literally means 'ragged fiend'. By Shakespeare's day, it had taken on its tamer connotation of 'street urchin'.

Nowadays, someone dismissed as a **toady** is a sycophant, a person who will do pretty much anything to earn a superior's approval. Perhaps unbelievably, the word genuinely has a connection with toads.

In the early nineteenth century, quack doctors (see CHARLATAN) would employ an impoverished person – usually a starving man who would do absolutely anything to earn a crust – to help them sell their so-called remedies. Typically the unfortunate person would have to consume an apparently poisonous toad in front of a gathering, so that the doctor could then prove his credentials by curing him. Naturally the toad was not poisonous in the first place, or else the poor patient – or 'toady' – would have died on the spot. Death was evidently a marginally less appealing prospect than being forced to eat a live creature, and a disgusting one at that, in public, and all for the sake of a small payment – with any luck something else to wash down the taste of toad.

A **dunce** is someone who displays a lack of understanding and an inability or unwillingness to learn anything. It is traditionally applied to school children, although I am finding as I get older that many adults suffer from the same affliction.

It is perhaps surprising to learn that a word we apply to the wilfully or unintentionally ignorant has an academic origin. John Duns Scotus was a Scottish philosopher, theologian and Catholic priest from around the turn of the fourteenth century. NICKNAMED 'Doctor Subtilis' and later considered one of the twelve greatest minds of his generation, Scotus's radical (for the time) ideas about the nature of existence were a significant influence on leading Catholics of the day, including Pope Boniface VIII. During his lifetime, Scotus collected an army of loyal followers who accepted his reasoning without question, and who were famously unable or unwilling to consider rational argument or opinions differing from their own. These people became known as *dunses*, later 'dunces'.

Probably one of my favourite words, **scallywag** is often used in the north of England, particularly around the Liverpool area (see also SCOUSE), to describe a boisterously energetic young male with little respect for authority. The original meaning is almost exactly the same. The word was originally 'scurryvag', thought by many to be a merging of the words 'scurrilous' and 'vagrant' but actually inspired by the Latin *scurra vagus*, 'wandering fool'. The word had evolved

231

into 'scallywag' by the time it was applied to the troublemakers around the Liverpool docks.

Posh is a word used by the British to describe the upper classes, although we might also admire a 'posh car' or a 'posh house' – basically, a swanky one, no matter who it belongs to. Rather amusingly, we also tend to call a certain footballer's wife 'Posh', which of course is a bit of an oxymoron.

We all know the popular theory about the origin of this word: how early passengers on the P&O (Peninsular and Orient, in case you were wondering) Steam Navigation Company had the option, if they were prepared to pay for it, of staying in the most comfortable cabins – identified as those on the shady port side on the way east to India, and those on the shady starboard side on the way back. These prestigious tickets were therefore stamped with the initials POSH: 'Port Out, Starboard Home'.

But I am suspicious of this explanation, for two reasons. Firstly, it was a drummer who first told me that story, and you don't expect to hear anything intelligent from a drummer. And secondly, it just isn't credible. For a start, not every journey began in Britain: thousands of people living or stationed in India would be doing the journey in reverse, so to speak, to visit the Motherland for a whole range of reasons. So their tickets – as well as the tickets of British people crossing the Atlantic to America, another route I've heard in connection with this theory – would presumably have been stamped SOPH: 'Starboard Out, Port Home'. And nobody has ever claimed that. Then, of course, before the Suez Canal was opened in 1869, all ships headed due south around the Cape of Good Hope, and then virtually due north again towards India – into and away from the sun respectively – meaning it wouldn't matter which side of the boat you were on: there was no avoiding getting roasted in the heat.

Despite it being a great story, and even despite *Chitty Chitty Bang Bang* (1968) featuring a song called 'Posh' ('Port out, starboard home, posh with a capital POSH'), there simply isn't a shred of evidence to support this theory. Sadly there isn't a single surviving ticket stamped 'POSH', and to top it all, P&O themselves dismiss the story.

Instead, it is far more likely that the word evolved from the Old ROMANY language, which itself originated in northern India, and was used to mean 'half'. A *posh-houri* was a halfpenny and *posh-kooroona* half a crown. In the London underworld, *posh-houri* became a slang term for money, so it is easy to see how the word 'posh' evolved over a couple of centuries from meaning 'half' to 'someone with money'. (Another erroneous story that has lingered on for decades but which doesn't merit space in this book is the one about 'golf' standing for 'gentlemen only, ladies forbidden'. It just doesn't.)

A **dude** was originally a well-dressed, savvy urban male living in one of the growing cities on the East Coast of America during the late nineteenth century. At least that's what the dudes choose to believe. Its original meaning was actually quite derogatory, used by Jonathan Periam in his book *The Home Farm and Manual* (1884) to describe narrow-minded but ostentatious city-dwellers (see also COCKNEY). And, perhaps surprisingly, it was these maligned individuals who took the word 'dude' over to what is now its spiritual home, the American West Coast.

Periam's inclusion of the word in his book reflects a wider usage. Towards the end of the nineteenth century, enterprising cattle-ranch owners began to offer wealthy Easterners the 'full cowboy experience', and city-dwellers flocked to spend their holidays on genuine working ranches. These 'guest ranches' grew in popularity as the railways expanded and provided a nostalgic, but safe, experience of the (by then) romanticised Wild West. The ranches soon became known as 'dude ranches', their paying guests being the dudes in question.

Now, one little-known fact about America is its widespread German influence, especially in the west of the country, following a considerable influx of Germans during the nineteenth century. (The US Federal Census of 2000 confirmed that, with 42 million members, the German-American community is the largest ethnic group in the country. Famous German Americans, you may be interested to know, include Donald Trump, Sandra Bullock and Leonardo DiCaprio.) Many of these immigrants were farmers, who used their skills to turn vast areas of barren land into productive farmland and cattle ranches. All of which means that German influence in the early days of Western settlement would have been significant. So when we turn back to the word 'dude', used to describe well-dressed visitors from the Eastern towns such as New York and Boston, who were presumably ill-equipped for farming or ranch life, we can see how the German dialect word *Dude*, 'idiot' or 'fool', might have played a part. Now that's the way to treat your customers.

Popinjay is a pejorative term, now rather old-fashioned, for an arrogant and probably empty-headed man, the sort of fellow Joseph Conrad had in mind when he wrote, in his short story 'The End of the Tether' (1902), 'When he looked around his club he saw only conceited popinjays who are too selfish to think of making a good woman happy.' Well, we can't have that, can we?

William Shakespeare popularised the word in *Henry IV, Part 1* (1597), in which Hotspur laments: 'I then, all smarting with my wounds being cold, / To be so pestered with a popinjay, / Out of my grief and my impatience, / Answered neglectingly I know not what.' Back in those days, it seems to have described an annoying, talkative person (see also CHATTERBOX).

Little wonder, then, that the word's probable origin is the Spanish word *papagayo*, 'parrot'. 'Popinjay' was in use by the end of the fourteenth century, referring to a target, quite possibly in the form of a parrot, placed on a post and used by archers for shooting practice. In Scotland, 'popinjay' is the art of shooting an arrow vertically, directly above your head, to dislodge a bird from a nest or branch. The sport was first recorded in the late fifteenth century and such shooting tournaments are still held today (no longer with live birds as the target, I should add, in case any RSPB members are reading this). Around the same time, the annual Festival of the Popinjay began as a British summertime tradition. Held on the first Sunday in May, the object of the festival was for archers to shoot at a rope from which a parrot effigy was suspended, with the first man to release the bird from its traumatic ordeal declared 'Captain Popinjay'.

A **Yankee** or **Yank** is US and European slang for an American. Originally the Native Americans used the words *yengeese, yanghis* and *yankees* (thought to be their way of saying 'English', or imitative of the popular Dutch name Janke, 'Johnny') to refer to European settlers. James Fenimore Cooper's novel *The Last of the Mohicans* (1826) includes the line: 'In what manner will he speak . . . when the runners count to him the scalps which five nights ago grew on the heads of the Yengeese?'

By the early eighteenth century, Dutch settlers were calling anybody living in the New World a Yankee, and the NICKNAME stuck. As early as 1713, Jonathan Hastings, a farmer in Cambridge, New York, was using it to describe his products as 'genuine American-made' and of the highest quality: 'Yankee Butter, the best in the world . . . Yankee leather, the best available', etc. During the War of Independence (1775–83), British soldiers used 'Yankee' as an insult against their enemy, whom they perceived to be dumb, simple farmer boys (see also JERK), but nobody in America regards the word as an insult these days. Far from it: it remains a term of national pride, as the popular New York Yankees baseball team demonstrates.

The **hippies** emerged in San Francisco, California, in the mid-1960s, as a counter-culture student movement of peace activists and anti-Vietnam War demonstrators. Calling themselves 'freaks', as they were described in the national media at the time, they were NICKNAMED hippies by the older **beatniks** or members of the Beat Generation, which included 1950s writers Jack Kerouac, Alan Ginsberg and William Burroughs. The nickname derives from **hipsters**, as the beatniks, who were idolised by the younger generation for their own counter-culture, were themselves sometimes known, in a nod to one of their own idols, popular JAZZ musician Harry Gibson, who adopted the stage name Harry the Hipster in 1940.

Gibson was in turn borrowing from African-American jazz slang dating back to the late nineteenth century, which included words such as 'hip', 'jive', 'swing', 'dig' and 'cool'. 'Hip' is thought to have come originally from the word *hipi*, 'to open one's eyes', from the Wolof language that is widely spoken across Western Africa, the homeland of many of those transported to America as slaves. In the jazz scene, it was more loosely translated as 'in the know' or 'up to date': anybody who was hip was a cool DUDE.

Unlike 'hippies', 'Beat Generation' was a name invented by members of that movement, who used the term widely in their own literature, alluding to the romantic idea that they were the post-war 'beaten' and lost generation. Although I imagine they were quickly found again when the Internal Revenue Service starting looking at their book sales figures.

What we now call a **dogsbody** was originally used in reference to a junior officer in the Royal Navy who carried out the unpopular tasks the senior officers disdained to do. The word evolved from the NICKNAME sailors gave their staple food, which was boiled peas in a bag, or pease pudding. What they called 'dog's body' we would probably nowadays term 'dog food'. Although the word has been used in reference to skivvies since the eighteenth century, it has not always been a derogatory expression. During the Second World War, RAF fighter pilot Douglas Bader, who flew in the Battle of Britain despite having lost both his legs in an acrobatic accident in 1931, used 'Dogsbody' as his military call-sign.

Dog days, incidentally, which are the hottest days of the year, are not in any way connected to dogsbodies or the DOG WATCH. Instead their name relates to the star Sirius, known as the Dog Star because it is the brightest in the constellation Canis Major, 'Greater Dog'. The ancient Greeks and the

Romans both noted how the Dog Star always rose on the hottest days of the year, leading to the expression 'dog days'.

Why do the English call the French **Frogs**, which are, according to Ambrose Bierce's satirical dictionary of 1911, 'reptiles with edible legs'? Mildly derogatory in English, the term is considered something of an insult by the French, who are certainly thin-skinned about it. Jean-David Levitte, the French Ambassador to the United States between 2002 and 2007, recently complained about talk show host David Letterman's use of the word: 'When you insult the French people simply because they are French, then it is a kind of racist campaign.' Which seems a little over-sensitive, doesn't it, even for a 'cheese-eating surrender monkey' (thanks, *Simpsons*)?

The obvious explanation for this NICKNAME is the worldwide belief that the French love eating frogs' legs. While this used to be true, France banned commercial frog farming in 1977, and since the creatures now have to be imported from Indonesia, Vietnam and China, their appearance on menus is now much rarer than it once was. Another theory is that British soldiers coined the expression during the Second World War when they first observed, to their horror, their French allies eating the reptiles. But the frog-eating theory seems a little lazy to me.

Some etymologists trace the word back to the first king of the Franks, Clovis I (466–511), who supposedly displayed images of frogs and bees upon his royal robes, but while this story is widely repeated, there is no evidence on statues, carvings or paintings to support it. Rather more verifiable is the line in Fanny Burney's debut novel *Evelina* (1778): 'Hark at you, Mrs Frog, you may lie in the mud till some of your Monsieurs come to help you out of it', which would seem to indicate a French/Frog connection dating back to long before the Second World War. Indeed, Queen Elizabeth I is said to have given her one-time suitor the Duke of Anjou, son of Henry II of France, the affectionate nickname 'my frog': his family displayed the little reptile on its heraldry, and it is said that he once gave the Virgin Queen a pair of frog-shaped earrings.

But the King of France's frogs go back slightly further than the reign of Elizabeth I. A popular folk song of 1549 entitled 'The Frog Came to the Myl Dur' (better known as 'Froggie Went A-Courting'), which appeared in Robert Wedderburn's *The Complaynt of Scotland*, recounts the tale of a frog wooing a mouse. The song is believed to be a reference to contemporary history and marriage between a French king (the frog) and a Scottish queen (the mouse). Two years before, in 1547, a battle had taken place between Henry VIII and the Scottish queen consort, Mary of Guise. When she turned to her allies in France for assistance, the French king, Henry II, proposed to unite the two countries against the English by marrying his three-year-old son Francis to Mary's daughter Princess Mary, the future infamous Queen of Scots. So it would seem that, thanks to an old Scottish folksong, the English have been calling the French 'Frogs' for nigh on 500 years.

To **jerk** something is to pull or yank it roughly. A 'jerk', meanwhile, is slang for an insignificant or inferior person. Two jerks are best avoided.

To locate the origin of the second definition we need to go back to the early nineteenth century and the spread of America's ambitious railway network, which cut its way through vast and previously uncharted territory. But this new form of travel created some practical problems, the principal of them being that steam engines needed water to power them. Initially this was provided by large troughs at the trackside every forty or fifty miles, from which the driver could 'jerk' water into the tank of the engine as he passed by. But as more and more people migrated to the West, tiny HICK towns with their own stations sprang up along the lines.

These remote outposts would also house vast water tanks from which passing trains could refill, as a result of which they were soon NICKNAMED 'jerkwater towns' by the railway companies. This in turn led to the rural inhabitants earning the moniker 'jerks', which developed over time into a derogatory term for the perceived simple-mindedness of country folk. By the end of the nineteenth century, the word was commonplace among inhabitants of the supposedly sophisticated East Coast of America. It was exported to Great Britain by YANKEE soldiers during the First and Second World Wars, and was often applied to rural British lads in much the same way.

The word 'jerk' was originally recorded in around 1550, meaning 'to stroke with a whip', taking us back to the first definition and showing how far the second definition has departed from it. Jerk beef, or beef **jerky**, is not connected to either definition, however, having evolved independently from the Quechua tribes of South America, whose word for meat that is cut into strips and then sun-dried is *echarqui*.

Bastard is a word that can be used in many effective ways. It appears to have been popularised by William Shakespeare, who plays around with the term in *King Lear* (1606), associating it with the similar-sounding 'base'. Edmund, the illegitimate son of the Earl of Gloucester, declaims: 'Why bastard? wherefore base? . . . Why brand they us / With base? with baseness? bastardy? base, base?'

'Bastard' has no connection etymologically with 'base', however. It is believed to have evolved from the Old French expression *fils de bast*, 'the son of a pack saddler' or indeed of any other long-distance traveller who passed through towns and villages, making the most of the local delicacies on offer and quickly disappearing before anyone could file a paternity suit. William the Conqueror (1028–87), the first Norman king of England, was known as 'William the Bastard' – and not only by the Anglo-Saxons he defeated at Hastings. In Normandy any illegitimate son of a nobleman was known as 'the bastard', pre-dating Shakespeare's usage by five centuries.

243

Australians, on the other hand, generally use the word as a term of affection, but then they have never really got to grips with the English language (see POMMY). These days, the word is rarely, if ever, used to describe an illegitimate child, but instead has found a happy home in football stadiums, where it is often prefixed with the word 'cheating'. Although not by me, you understand.

An **ignoramus** is somebody of low or no intelligence. The word has been in common use in England since the seventeenth century, although perhaps surprisingly it started out as a legal expression. Like much of our legal language, 'ignoramus' is derived from Latin, in which it means 'we don't know'. The word, translated as 'we take no notice of it' in a legal context, would traditionally be stamped on legal documents rejected by the courts as badly thought out and without basis.

The original **jackanapes**, which we use in modern times to describe an impertinent person as a monkey (or ape), was William de la Pole (1396–1450), the 1st Duke of Suffolk, who was unfairly blamed for some of England's defeats during the later stages of the Hundred Years' War with France (1337–1453). Early in his career, de la Pole had been a respected soldier: he was badly injured at the Siege of Harfleur in 1415, but went on to inherit his elder brother's titles when the latter was killed at Agincourt a few months

244

later. William later became co-commander of the English forces during the Siege of Orleans in 1429, which was famously relieved by Joan of Arc. Beaten by a girl, he went on the run but was soon captured and held prisoner by Charles VII of France until he was ransomed in 1431.

Back in England, de la Pole continued to rise up the ranks at court, becoming Lord High Admiral of England in 1447. This move marked the downturn in his fortunes, however: over the next three years, England lost nearly all of her possessions in France, which had taken over 100 years of war to accumulate. Imprisoned in the Tower of London and given the NICKNAME Jack the Ape, or Jack Napes, largely because his family crest depicted a tame ape wearing a ball and chain, the unfortunate de la Pole was banished to France, of all places, although his ship was intercepted at sea and he was murdered by one of his growing number of enemies.

An **anorak**, to most people nowadays, is someone with a keen interest in subjects that the majority of us fail to comprehend, or simply have no desire to (see also GEEKS). A cricket fan obsessed with statistics could be described as an anorak, as could anybody who brightens our lives with dull and detailed trivia about stamps or coins. An anorak is also, of course, a waterproof jacket with a hood, commonly worn by people with fascinating outdoor hobbies such as bird watching, train spotting or fishing – which, by the way, if it weren't for the rod, could otherwise be known as 'sitting by the river all day looking like an idiot'. Traditionally, anoraks who enjoy anorak-wearing pursuits speak in their own unique nasal tone, regardless of where they come from, and congregate on the same day every month in associations or clubs to share their enthusiasm with like-minded people.

The original anorak was imported into the English language, and on to the downstairs coat rack, in 1924, long after it was discovered that the Inuit of Greenland kept warm and dry in hooded waterproof coats that were made from seal skin and called *anoraqs*. By the 1950s, they were being made out of a rather more prosaic material, nylon, and following a feature article in *Vogue* they became something of a fashion item.

There are several suggestions for why the word 'anorak' became associated with special-interest groups, the most compelling being that it was coined by a radio presenter working for Radio Caroline. The pirate radio station, which broadcast from a ship in the North Sea, became so popular in the late 1960s that particularly devoted listeners would charter boats and sail out to visit the presenters and crew. These visits became so common that when, on a cold rainy day in 1974, three boatloads of fans arrived, disc jockey Andy Archer decided to present his programme from the deck instead of the studio, to give everybody something to see. When his programme went live, he announced to thousands of listeners that he was 'delighted to see so many anoraks on board', giving a new NICKNAME to enthusiastic fans of pirate radio stations and other cultish hobbies.

Parkas, incidentally, were originally developed for the United States military and issued to servicemen stationed in very cold countries, long before the London Mods (Modernists) made them part of their clothing culture. The word *parka* is the Nenet (northern Russian) dialect word for 'animal skin' and was first recorded by the English travel writer Samuel Purchas in 1625.

Geeks and **nerds** are closely associated with ANORAKS, although there are two very clear differences. Firstly, their activities will always be of a highly technical nature and secondly, more often than not, their obscure passion for the unfathomable will also be the subject of their studies or their employment. In other words, they are professional anoraks.

'Geek' is an American slang word that was defined in the 1954 edition of *Webster's New International Dictionary of the English Language* as 'a carnival wild man whose act usually includes biting the head off a snake or chicken'. That sounds more like Ozzy Osbourne to me and I wouldn't call him a geek (to his face). But this carnival definition is a relatively modern one, deriving – as does the more conventional definition – from the obsolete English word *geck*, 'fool', which came from the Dutch *gek*, 'very silly'. Hang on, perhaps that does describe Ozzy after all.

Nerds have much in common with geeks and share a spiritual leader in His Nerdship Bill Gates, founder of Microsoft Corporation and high priest of the technical world. There are various theories for the origin of the word, many of them rather nerd-like themselves. In the 1960s, for example, free-spirited students supposedly used the word 'knurd', which is 'drunk' backwards, to denote those unusual scholars who actually studied something during their time at university. Another claim is that Mortimer Snerd, a popular but slow-witted ventriloquist's dummy used by Edgar Bergen in the 1930s, had something to do with it. The second theory is perhaps more plausible given that the first printed instance of 'nerd' came in 1950, in Dr Seuss's *If I Ran the Zoo*: 'I'll sail to Ka-Troo / And bring back an It-Kutch, a Preep and a Proo, / A Nerkle, a Nerd and a Seersucker too!'

Other suggested origins include the 1940s American slang word *nurt*, meaning 'crazy', which later developed into 'nut', and the Northern Electric Research and Development (NERD) laboratory in Ottawa. It would seem that there were just far too many nerds around in the mid-twentieth century for us to be able to settle on one watertight etymology. But whatever the correct origin, we have the worldwide hit sitcom *Happy Days* to thank for making 'nerd' part of our English language in the 1970s, as it was used extensively by the Fonz to describe his studious friends.

We nowadays tend only to hear the word **Yahoo** in connection with the search engine and email provider of the same name (see also GOOGLE). But from the mid-eighteenth century onwards, 'yahoo' was a common term for a THUG (see also HOODLUM, LARRIKIN, RUFFIAN). Is there any connection between the two? Interestingly enough, there is.

In the last part of *Gulliver's Travels*, Jonathan Swift's satirical novel of 1726, Gulliver describes a voyage to the country of the Houyhnhnms, a race of intelligent horses who rule over their humanoid but brutish compatriots, the Yahoos. The Yahoos are a constant threat to the harmony of the land. Although Gulliver resembles the horses in intellect, they are unable to disassociate him from his grotesque human appearance, and banish him to live with 'his own people'. Thanks to the novel's popularity, 'yahoo' quickly came to be synonymous with 'thug'.

When David Filo and Jerry Yang were looking for a new name for their pioneering internet search facility in 1994 – hardly surprising since the original one, 'David and Jerry's Guide to the World Wide Web', hadn't exactly tripped off the tongue – they scoured the dictionary and came across 'yahoo', whose meaning, 'rude, unsophisticated and uncouth', they felt summed them up.

More recently in Australia, and no doubt influenced by *Gulliver's Travels*, 'Yahoo' is a name given to a large mythical, hairy part-man, part-simian creature supposed to have inhabited the remote parts of the east of the country. I use the word 'mythical' loosely here as I realise the description could well describe any Australian male.

In the parts of England popular with 'staycationers', the natives have adopted their very own derogatory terms for the home-grown tourists who flock in annually, much to their annoyance. The West Country and the Lake District are among the favoured destinations, but far from welcoming their visitors with open arms, as vital additions to the local economy, most natives follow the time-honoured British tradition of expressing resentment. To be fair, I probably wouldn't be best pleased either if I couldn't drive down my own road because it was stuffed full of **emmets** (tourists) in their **grockle shells** (caravans) or **grockle cans** (tourist coaches).

'Grockle' and 'emmet' are both dismissive words for 'tourist', 'emmet' being an old West Country dialect word for 'ant', there being an obvious parallel with the hordes of tourists who drive up from the cities every summer and swarm all over the countryside and take over the beaches.

Any ant who has taken a holiday in these areas of the country, and I am one of them, knows that 'service' in a restaurant or hotel appears to be a mere inconvenience between taking the booking and collecting the cash. Generally speaking, the locals who grudgingly accept grockles as a necessary evil have no idea how the word became associated with 'tourists' and assume there must be a connection with 'grockle', a commercially worthless shellfish that breeds in abundance around the coastline and which damages, or clogs up, fishermen's nets and pots. The poor hard-working fisherman then has to spend most of his time clearing the valueless grockles away. It's a good theory but sadly there is no shellfish called a grockle. Perhaps people are confusing it with the cockle?

The alternative explanation for this derisive term is more elaborate, but still quite unconvincing. It centres around Charles Adrien Wettach (1880–1959), a Swiss-born composer, musician and music-hall clown who in 1903 adopted the stage name 'Grock'. By the time of the outbreak of the First World War, Grock's fame had spread throughout Europe. As hostilities increased, he fled to Britain where he remained until 1924, performing around the country for both British and American troops, and later the general public. He then left for America, where his fame quickly spread. By 1954, the world's most famous clown was able to retire in a luxurious fifty-room lakeside villa in Italy. His contribution to the world of entertainment is recognised by the Grock d'Or, an annual award for young circus artists.

What has this to do with the West Country, you ask? Well, some of the natives argue that the word they use associates tourists with clowns. As I said, unconvincing. But 'grockle' was certainly in use shortly after Grock's heyday:

Michael Winner's 1964 film *The System*, which is set in the West Country, features frequent use of the word in reference to out-of-towners.

A **nipper** is a small child: usually a boy, but girls can be nippers too. *Brewer's Dictionary of Phrase and Fable* describes 'nipper' as a slang word for 'small boy', so called because 'he is "nippy", or swift and agile'. The first nippers were recorded in around 1530, when the streets of London were teeming with young orphans who either grouped together or were gathered up by the unscrupulous, given shelter and forced to 'work' (often in the form of stealing and other petty crime). Charles Dickens later illustrated this perfectly in his iconic second novel, *Oliver Twist* (1838). By Dickens's time, young thieves had been known as 'nippers' for centuries (see also WHIPPERSNAPPER). If caught, they were subject to the same harsh punishment as adults, including whipping, transportation or even a death sentence. In 1814, five nippers under the age of fourteen were hanged at the Old Bailey, the youngest being only eight years old. With all this in mind, it is no surprise that the word 'nipper' evolved from the Middle English *nyppe*, 'to steal'.

The origin of the current expression could equally well be nautical, however. In sailing terms, 'nippers' are the small lines that were historically 'nipped' to a large ship's anchor warps or cables to make them easier to handle. The job of attaching the lines was a task given to the young cabin boys, the 'nippers'.

There are two well-known explanations for the word **chav**. One is that the letters are an acronym used by the police to describe a miscreant as 'Council House And Violent', while the other is that it is a short form of '**Ch**eltenham **av**erage', used by pupils at the upmarket Cheltenham Ladies College to describe inferior local boys. But I imagine these both to be recent inventions for a word that has been in use for over 150 years. Another popular theory is that the word is somehow connected with girls from Chatham, but the evidence for this link is vague at best.

It's possible that the term comes from the northeast of England and the Geordie dialect word *charva*, indicating a rough, unruly child. Equally, it could be ROMANY in origin, from their word for 'boy', *chavo*. You can take your pick. But while we're on the subject of offensive slang names, you might be interested to know that the word **pikey**, applied to a GYPSY, is thought to derive from 'turnpike' – used for collecting tolls on the single road in and out of a town and hence passed regularly by travelling folk such as the Romanies.

A **Cockney** is traditionally a working-class Londoner 'born within the sound of Bow bells' – that is, the bells of St Mary-le-Bow in Cheapside, a few hundred yards from

St Paul's Cathedral. In Dick Whittington's day, the bells could be heard from as far away as Highgate, but given that Cheapside is now in a noisy, built-up commercial district not known for its maternity hospitals, there must surely be very few genuine modern-day Cockneys around. (The bells can in fact be heard from Guy's Hospital south of the Thames, but I'm not sure many south Londoners actually want to be called Cockneys.)

The reality is that anyone born in any English city or large town is a Cockney, since 'cokeney' (from the fourteenth-century word for a hen's egg) was once a term of derision for city-dwellers who looked completely out of place in the countryside (see also DUDE). So next time you wander into a quiet rural pub and the locals give you that 'Not from around 'ere' look, simply admit loudly and proudly that you are a Cockney. I'm sure they'll understand.

Nowadays, Liverpudlians are quite proud to call themselves **scousers**, a NICKNAME derived from the local dish, **scouse**. Given how specifically Liverpool-related the word is, it is interesting to discover that it comes from Norway, specifically a Norwegian stew – *lapskaus* – imported by Scandinavian sailors in the eighteenth century. The name of the dish was subsequently corrupted to *lobs course*, *lobscouse* and finally 'scouse', which, rather like other food-based nicknames for a group of people, such as LIMEY and Kraut (from 'sauerkraut'), soon became attached to the good folk of Liverpool (see also SCALLYWAG).

We are all prone to being **loafers** from time to time. In fact, I regard loafing as something of a hobby of mine. Experts in these matters have even identified different types of loafing, including 'social loafing', defined in an article in 1993 as 'the reduction in motivation and effort when individuals work as part of a group'. This is known more informally as the Sucker Effect, in which an individual does his darnedest not to exert himself unduly, in the belief that the rest of the group will do his work for him. According to psychologists, this is a bad thing.

Many people have tried to get to the bottom of this phenomenon. In 1913, a French professor named Max Ringelmann did a series of experiments with tug-of-war teams, measuring rope strain and pull force in various scenarios. He was fascinated to discover that the group pulls never matched the sum total of the individual pulls; in some cases the sum total of an eight-man effort only equalled the sum of four individual pulls, proving that members of a team applied only half the force they did when tested as individuals. He concluded that 'When employing a man, or draft animals, better use is achieved when the source of motive power works alone.'

So it seems I didn't invent loafing after all, although I have certainly turned it into an art form. The 'loafer', social or otherwise, was first identified in America in the 1820s. The word evolved from the now obsolete German *Landläufer*, literally 'land runner' but used to indicate a vagabond or tramp. It became 'landloafer' in Britain, to describe the same type of person, before finally turning into 'loafer', to describe me.

Pommy, or **Pom**, is well-known Australian slang for an Englishman. The word is often preceded by the words 'useless' or 'whingeing', and suffixed by BASTARDS, particularly when it comes to sporting prowess – or lack of. Former Australian rugby captain David Campese made headlines during the 2003 Rugby World Cup, when he supposedly declared that the 'Poms would win nothing', words that came back to bite him when England beat Australia in the final.

The expression supposedly arises from the acronym POME, which stands for 'Prisoner Of Mother England', or alternatively from POHM, 'Prisoner Of His/Her Majesty'. Either way, it was a name given to the English convicts who were transported to Australia in the eighteenth and nineteenth centuries, and who were not natives of that country. So basically, if you are not an ABORIGINE living in Australia then you are a Pommy.

D. H. Lawrence, one of the great novelists of his generation, had an alternative theory, however. He suggested in his 1923 novel *Kangeroo* that the expression evolved from the pomegranate and the red, florid appearance of the fruit, which he claimed matched that of the traditional complexion of the British after three months on the high seas. But I respectfully suggest that the great man made that up.

In America, the slang term for an Englishman is a **Limey** (see also GROG, POMMY), which is sometimes used with affection and at other times disparagingly. The name harks back to 1795, when the Royal Navy began to issue fresh limes and other citrus fruit to the fleet as a means of preventing scurvy (a measure pioneered by Admiral Vernon earlier in the century – see GROG), which is caused by a lack of vitamin C and which historically affected sailors on long voyages. As a result, British sailors became known as 'Lime Juicers' or 'Limeys', a NICKNAME that has stuck in the United States.

On land, scurvy was known as the 'spring disease' as it usually occurred after a long winter when people had little or no access to fresh fruit and vegetables. This is also one reason why children are traditionally given oranges in their Christmas stockings, as an attempt to combat spring disease.

Gorblimey is the sort of word my granddad would have used when he saw something he wasn't expecting. 'Blimey' was first recorded in Barrère and Leland's *Dictionary of Slang, Jargon and Cant*, first published in 1889. Three years earlier, Arthur Morrison had used the expression in his most popular novel, *A Child of the Jago*, depicting life in the East End of London. 'Gorblimey', or 'corblimey', is essentially a London word (see also COCKNEY) and a euphemism for the expression 'God blind me', which had become an established part of the English language long before James Joyce used the line 'God blimey if she ain't a clinker' in his landmark novel *Ulysses* (1922).

Bollocks is a good old Anglo–Saxon word of Germanic origin, which is nowadays used mainly as a relatively mild swearword but technically just means 'testicles' (see also AVOCADO, KNACKER). In both senses of the word, it somehow only sounds correct when said with a British accent.

Perhaps surprisingly, the word appears in John Wycliffe's 1382 translation of the Bible, in which we learn that: 'Al beeste that kitt and taken a wey the ballokes is, ye shulen not offre to the Lord.' Which translates into modern English as: 'Any beast that has had its bollocks taken away [been castrated] should not be offered as a sacrifice to the Lord.' By the eighteenth century, 'bollocks' and its close cousin 'ballocks' had somehow become slang terms for 'clergyman', suggesting that what some of them preached from the pulpit perhaps led to the NICKNAME.

One of the most versatile old words in the English language, 'bollocks' can also be used as an expression of dismay or frustration – 'Oh, bollocks' – or a term of appreciation: 'That really is the bollocks.' The word's most exciting role in its very long history, however, was at the centre of a notorious court case in relatively recent times.

In 1977, the Sex Pistols ruffled a few establishment feathers with the release of their debut punk rock album, *Never Mind the Bollocks, Here's the Sex Pistols*. The band and the manager of a Nottingham record shop who had dared to display the album in his window were immediately sued. The high-profile defence lawyer John Mortimer QC, creator of *Rumpole of the Bailey*, successfully demonstrated that the word 'bollocks' had for centuries been in common use as slang for a 'priest', and that it usually simply meant 'nonsense'. The court was forced to publicly concede that the word was not to be considered obscene. Although admittedly other words for 'nonsense' (see under CLAPTRAP) may not have had quite the same ring.

FOREIGN LANGUAGES

The British Raj had a major influence on the English language in the nineteenth and early twentieth centuries. The four main dialects of Southeast Asia are, in no particular order, Urdu, Hindi, Tamil and Sanskrit, and all of them have contributed words to the melting pot of different languages that make up English.

Your grandmother's **bungalow**, for instance, could not look more quaint and traditionally English, but the original bungalows weren't inhabited by British pensioners but by English sailors who, during the late seventeenth century, were billeted in small, single-STOREY units at the port of Bengal. Referred to as *bangla* (literally 'belonging to Bengal'), these buildings were no better than hovels, but under British occupation over the coming centuries grand and spacious single-storey 'bungalows', as they came to be known, were built for Empire officials and visiting dignitaries. As the British began to move out of the cramped industrial cities during the nineteenth century, more land was made available in the countryside and single-storey living became an established way of life.

Other Indian-inspired 'English' words include **veranda**, a Hindi and Urdu word for 'courtyard'; **loot**, from the Hindi *lut* and Sanskrit *lunth*, 'to rob'; **dinghy**, meaning *dingi* or 'rowing boat' in Hindi; **bangle**, from *bangli*, Hindi for 'glass bracelet'; **shampoo**, from the Hindi *campo*, 'press' (in the sense of a massage); and **khaki**, from the Urdu *kaki*, 'dust-coloured'. (See also DOOLALLY, KARMA, PUKKA, POLO, PUNDIT, SWASTIKA, THUG.)

In the way of clothing, we have **bandana**, from the Hindi *bandhna*, 'to tie'; **pyjamas**, from *paijaamaa*, Hindi for 'leg clothing'; and **cummerbund**, from the Urdu *karmarband* for a waist binding; not to mention JODPHURS. While from the culinary world we have **chutney**, from the Hindi *catni*, a type of spicy side dish, and some much older words, dating back several centuries before the Raj. These include the indispensable **curry** from the Tamil *kari*; **mango** – while we're talking chutney – from *manga*, a Portuguese word but derived originally from an Indian one; and of course **rice**, which has come to us on a particularly tortuous journey via Old French, Italian, Latin and Greek, but which is ultimately from the Sanskrit *vrihi*.

It should come as no surprise that the language of our Irish neighbours has influenced modern English in many colourful ways. (For words covered under their own entries, see BLARNEY, BOYCOTT, PHONEY, SHENANIGANS, SMITHEREENS, STEEPLECHASE.) According to Irish legend, a *bean sidhe*, which we pronounce **banshee**, is a 'woman of the fairy mounds'– a female spirit from underground who howls and screams at the windows of a house to alert the occupants that one of their number is close to death. In modern times, a banshee can be located in any English pub on a Friday evening, loudly announcing much the same thing to anyone unfortunate enough to be within earshot. **Gob**, while we're on the subject of the overly talkative, apparently comes from the Gaelic for 'beak' or 'mouth', and **slapper** from *slapach*, which translates as 'slovenly' or 'dirty (prostitute)' (see also BIMBO, FLOOZIE).

But Ireland's greatest contribution to world culture must surely be **whiskey**, originally called *usquebaugh*, based on the Gaelic *uisce beatha*, 'water of life'. A **nip** of whiskey was once a 'nipperkin', which was a standard measure of wine, beer or spirits measuring about 280ml, approximately half a pint. Now that's what I call a nip.

Moving on, and just to annoy my many Irish friends, their traditional word **craic**, which basically means 'having a great time', actually has an English origin. The expression **having a crack**, meaning the same thing, was exported to Northern Ireland via the Ulster Scots and translated into Gaelic as recently as the 1950s. It was then popularised during the 1970s by radio chat-show host Seán Bán Breathnach, whose Irish-language programme was advertised with the promise that 'We will have music, chat and the craic'. In England and America a **wisecrack**, or a crack, has been a joke or a general good time since the nineteenth century, and to this day comedians are still **cracking** jokes to entertain their audiences.

Finally, the Irishness (or otherwise) of the word **kibosh** has been the subject of heated debate. To put the kibosh on something is to end it deliberately and definitively, or to prevent it from occurring in the first place. There are several claims as to the origin and history of this word, the most popular, and obvious, being that it comes from either Yiddish or Hebrew, but there is no solid evidence to support this. The notion that *chai*, the Hebrew for 'life', has ended up connected with the London slang word 'bosh', as has been suggested, seems a little unlikely. Another theory is that it comes from the Yiddish *kabas*, meaning 'to suppress', which some American etymologists believe to have evolved from the Arabic *qurbash*, a sort of whip. Meanwhile, in Ireland, the Gaelic word for the black cap a judge would wear when passing the death penalty is *cai bais*, pronounced 'ky-bawsh', which is perhaps rather more plausible since putting one of those on would certainly indicate the end of something.

But my favourite claim, also from Ireland, takes us to the city of Cork, whose Coal Quay was home to a legendary cabbage market between 1745 and 1914. The Gaelic word for 'cabbage' is *cabaiste*, pronounced 'ki-boshta'. For each

auction, a single cabbage from each lot was displayed on a bench for potential buyers to inspect. When the bidding was over, a hollow silver 'cabaiste' would be placed over the sample cabbage; in time, the end of each round of bidding became known as 'putting the cabaiste on it'. With cabbage being exported in great quantities across Europe, the expression travelled too – although the auctions themselves were abruptly halted at the start of the First World War when trade with continental Europe was halted. Sadly, I suspect there may be a touch of BLARNEY in the air here, since Cork's 'legendary' cabbage market is conspicuously absent from the history books.

The French have managed to work their way into our language, despite the historical enmity between our two nations. For example, **au pairs** may be surprised to learn that their late-Victorian counterparts were simply one half of an arrangement under which two parties provided services for one another 'on equal terms', with no money changing hands. The word has nothing to do with being assigned to a 'pair', as in a married couple. For anything **advantageous** we have the Old French *avantage* to thank, which means 'a circumstance favourable to success'. Perhaps one of the most unusual French imports is the exclamation we make when we sneeze – **atishoo** – which, believe it or not, is thought to be an anglicisation of the French version of 'bless you', *à tes souhaits*, which translates literally as 'to your wishes'.

There are far too many French–English words to enumerate and I've barely touched on the letter 'A', but here are a few of the most commonly used. (See also BOHEMIANS, GADGET, MAYONNAISE, PICNIC, ZEST.) From French cookery alone we have adopted enough terms to fill a dictionary. We could start with **à la carte**, choosing dishes 'according to the card' or **menu** ('detailed list'), from which we might select CANAPÉS and HORS D'OEUVRES, before moving on to the **entrées** and **desserts** (from *desservir*, 'clear the table'). Quality is always of the highest: **cordon bleu** is the 'blue ribbon' awarded to first-class chefs before the French Revolution, while **haute cuisine** is the kind of 'high cookery' they were known for. The French **gourmet** (originally 'wine taster') is a **connoisseur** ('knowledgeable person') of fine food and wine, the **crème de la crème** ('best of the cream') in his field. It's a shame that British cookery isn't good enough to warrant its own lexicon, but *c'est la vie* – which is not to be confused (as I have heard it done) with *Vive la France*.

It will come as no surprise to hear that Italian, like French, has had a huge influence on modern English, but there are now so many Italian words in our language that we can easily overlook their origin. **Gazette**, for instance, is a shortened version of *gazeta de la novità*, which translates from the Venetian dialect as 'halfpenny of news', since a *gazeta* was a low-value coin. **Mezzanine**, an additional floor between two main floors of a building, comes from *mezzano*, 'middle'. For other words covered under their own entries, see BALONEY, BIMBO, CHARLATAN, RUFFIAN.

But it is in two fields in particular that Italian has had the biggest impact internationally. The first is food. When your **pasta** ('paste', as in 'dough') is firm to the bite it is **al dente**, literally 'to the tooth', while a **pizza** is just a plain old 'pie'. Your morning **cappuccino** is named after the Capuchin monks whose traditional brown cape or hood (*cappuccino*) it resembles in colour. Your caffè **espresso** wouldn't sound quite so exotic if it was called 'pressed-out coffee', which is exactly what 'espresso' means; likewise a PICNIC 'in the fresh (air)' sounds considerably less romantic than one taken **alfresco**.

The second field is music, from which we have **forte**, 'strong' (as in loud), and **piano**, 'soft', combining to form **pianoforte**, an instrument that can produce a wide range of tone from soft to loud. To sing **solo** is to perform 'on your own'; to do it **sotto voce** is to sing 'under voice' or quietly. A **baritone** is a 'heavy tone', pitched between tenor and bass, an **alto** is a 'high' one and the **soprano** is the one 'above'. The **cello**, or violoncello, means 'little violone' in Italian, referring to the old viol family of stringed instruments, **trombone** comes from *tromba* ('trumpet') and **piccolo** means a 'small flute'. A **libretto** is the 'booklet' in which lyrics to an opera would be printed and **opera** simply translates as 'work'. The **tempo** is the 'timing', pretty indispensable in a piece of music, while the **concert** where you can hear all of this is an event at which musicians 'harmonise' (*concertare* in Italian).

The Yiddish language has been a great source of wonderful words in English; many of the most evocative and unusual terms we use have their root in Yiddish culture.

During the 1980s, an excellent word for an unpopular phenomenon swept through the housing industry: **gazumping**. This is when a seller accepts a last-minute offer that trumps one that has already been accepted, often effectively rendering the original would-be buyer homeless. The word comes from the Yiddish *gezumph*, 'to overcharge'. **Gazundering**, a later variant on 'gazumping', is the equally obnoxious practice of lowering a previously accepted bid during a falling market.

Other Yiddish words that have enriched our way of speaking include *beygl*, a dense ring-shaped bread roll, and *nashn*, meaning 'to greedily eat', which is why we might **nosh** down our **bagels** at lunchtime. *Khutspe* is the daring audacity we know as **chutzpah** and a **schlep**, from *shlepn*, 'to drag', is a long tiring journey. *Klots*, 'wooden block', gives us **klutz**, someone endowed with a similar level of intelligence and dexterity, while *shmok*, a certain part of the male anatomy, has given rise to **schmuck**, a 'fool'. We use **kosher** to indicate something genuine (see also PUKKA), the word deriving from the 'proper' way of preparing food in respect of Jewish dietary customs. When we're not in the mood for talking, we keep **schtum** or silent; alternatively, we **schmooze** or make small talk in order to win someone's trust or favour (see also BLARNEY). If we don't watch our words, however, we can find ourselves in a **schemozzle**, a muddle or even a brawl.

ACKNOWLEDGEMENTS

My first thanks must go to Paul and Gen Ryan for their hospitality this year, and likewise to Sheila and Tony Podmore. Peter Gordon is here again, largely because I find myself becoming more superstitious as the years go by, as well as Troy Kyle in Cape Town, who went out of his way to assist. Rebecca Younger should have a mention, too, for her enthusiastic support.

Special thanks go to everybody who works in bookshops up and down the land. I wonder how many writers and publishers fully realise that, without you, we wouldn't be employed – unless we took ourselves out to Sunday car-boot sales and flogged our books from the back of a van. I hope you, more than anybody, enjoy this one.

Big thanks to Robert Smith of the Robert Smith Literary Agency in London, and to the Random House team: Nigel Wilcockson, Silvia Crompton, Kate Parker, Rosie Gailer, and everyone else who has helped make this book. Thanks also to Ama and Grace Page for providing the fantastic illustrations once again.

Finally I would like to thank the students at my first writer's workshop in Cape Town: Eilat Aviram, Lisa Kane, John Gray, Joy Macnab, Catherine Riley, Sanaa Peterson, Troy Kyle, Hazel Brown, Colleen Beak, Joy Millar, Kendal Probert, Kim Van Reizig and all at Hippo Communications. Good luck to all of you.

INDEX OF ENTRIES